Wittgenstein

and the

Grammar

of

Literary

Experience

JAMES GUETTI

Wittgenstein and the Grammar of Literary Experience

The University of Georgia Press

Athens and London

Designed by Mary Mendell
Set in Joanna by Tseng Information Systems, Inc.
Printed and bound by Thomson Shore, Inc.
The paper in this book meets the guidelines for permanence and durability of the Committee on Production Guidelines for Book Longevity of the Council on Library Resources.
Printed in the United States of America
97 96 95 94 93 C 5 4 3 2 1

Library of Congress Cataloging in Publication Data
Guetti, James L.
Wittgenstein and the grammar of literary experience / James Guetti. p. cm.
Includes bibliographical references.
ISBN 0-8203-1496-X (alk. paper)
1. Language and languages—Philosophy. 2. Literature—Philosophy. 3. Wittgenstein, Ludwig, 1889–1951—Contributions in philosophy of language. I. Title.
P106.G796 1993
801—dc20 92-19181
CIP
British Library Cataloging in Publication Data available

This book is for *Anthony*,

to *be exact*

What is the use of talking,
and there is no end of talking,
There is no end of things in the heart.
—EZRA POUND, "Exiles Letter"

Contents

Acknowledgments

Without the help of William Dowling, this book would not have come to its present form. It was a stroke of luck for me that he became a colleague at a time when I was sorely in need of someone who understood what I was trying to do. Dowling not only shared my interests in Wittgenstein and in certain questions of literary theory but also had the philosophical awareness to make me refine them, and so from my conversations with him I got both the encouragement and the criticism I needed. But beyond this his actual reading of an earlier version of the book was of enormous help; I have never known anyone who could so willingly and arduously, and effectively, lend himself to another's work. And the fact that his doing so seemed genuinely to spring from his own literary and philosophic interests made it possible for me to accept it with at least some grace and really to use it.

I am also grateful to William Pritchard, for support of my work over the years above and beyond the call of friendship, and despite the differences in our ways of doing what we do: for he is able, as I am not and with an "untheoreticalness" that I admire, just to *describe*, as Wittgenstein says we must.

But the oldest debt I should acknowledge here is to two men, Theodore Baird and Armour Craig, who years ago at Amherst College first put to me questions that I have been trying to answer ever since, of which many of the questions asked in this book are the descendants.

Somehow, in some way, I must have thought back then that these questions, and the methods for addressing them that were implicit in the way they were framed, were good ones, even the right ones. I still think so. The best teaching lasts.

A few pages of this introduction first appeared, in somewhat different form, in my essay "Freudian Slippage" in *Raritan* 8, 1, and a section of "Wittgenstein and Literary Theory," published in *Raritan* 4, 1 and 4, 2, was reworked extensively—since my understanding of Wittgenstein had changed, and I hope improved, a good deal—for its place in chapter 1, Uses and Aspects. I thank the editors of *Raritan* for permission to use that material here. But I also want particularly to thank Richard Poirier and Thomas Edwards for the generosity with which they have always regarded my work.

Abbreviations for Works Frequently Cited

BB Ludwig Wittgenstein, *The Blue and Brown Books* (New York: Harper and Row, 1965).

CAL Maurice Merleau-Ponty, *Consciousness and the Acquisition of Language*, trans. Hugh J. Silverman (Evanston, Ill.: Northwestern University Press, 1973).

FTA Ernest Hemingway, *A Farewell to Arms* (New York: Scribners, 1929).

IL Sigmund Freud, *Introductory Lectures on Psychoanalysis*, trans. James Strachey (New York: Norton, 1966).

OC Ludwig Wittgenstein, *On Certainty*, trans. G. E. M. Anscombe and Denis Paul (New York: Harper and Row, 1972).

PEL Sigmund Freud, *The Psychopathology of Everyday Life*, trans. Alan Tyson (New York: Norton, 1960).

PI Ludwig Wittgenstein, *Philosophical Investigations*, trans. G. E. M. Anscombe (New York: Macmillan, 1968).

PP Robert Frost, *Poetry and Prose*, ed. Edward Lathem and Lawrance Thompson (New York: Holt, 1972).

RPP 1 Ludwig Wittgenstein, *Remarks on the Philosophy of Psychology*, vol. 1, trans. G. E. M. Anscombe (Chicago: University of Chicago Press, 1980).

RPP 2 ———, *Remarks on the Philosophy of Psychology*, vol. 2, trans. C. G. Luckhardt and M. A. E. Aue (Chicago: University of Chicago Press, 1980).

SAR Ernest Hemingway, *The Sun Also Rises* (New York: Scribners, 1926).

SF William Faulkner, *The Sound and the Fury* (New York: Vintage, 1984).

SLP Jacques Lacan, *Speech and Language in Psychoanalysis*, trans. Anthony Wilden (Baltimore: Johns Hopkins University Press, 1981).

SP John Crowe Ransom, *Selected Poems* (New York: Ecco Press, 1978).

STA William Empson, *Seven Types of Ambiguity* (New York: New Directions, 1966).

WS Wallace Stevens, *Collected Poems* (New York: Vintage, 1982).

Wittgenstein and the Grammar of Literary Experience

Introduction

"When we look into ourselves as we do in philosophy," Wittgenstein says, "we often get to see just such a picture. A full-blown pictorial representation of our grammar. Not facts; but as it were illustrated turns of speech" (PI, 295). He was not speaking at that moment, of course, of our "introspections" in literary studies, nor were literary or "aesthetic" matters ever his first concern. But I shall try to show in these discussions that what we get both from reading literature and from thinking about that reading, no matter how "inwardly" we think, is precisely a perception of "illustrated turns of speech," and it is a perception so powerful that we mistake its object for what we suppose must be more important to us—for "facts," as Wittgenstein suggests, or, as he suggests much more frequently, for *meanings*. "When we look into ourselves" about our literary experience, I shall maintain, what we are looking at is the language in us; our "imaginative life" is inseparably entwined with language and *its* life, and in our introspections we are focused on and brought up against just what we can say. Why this must be so, and, more importantly, why this apprehension of language is for us so powerful, so seductive, and—when we try to account for it—so confusing, are the questions that concern me here.

One of the reasons why Wittgenstein provides such a valuable access to these "literary" questions is that his philosophy privileges nothing above language; for him, all deeply philosophical questions are either questions about language or questions whose philosophic concern with the presumably "unverbal" is actually generated by linguistic confusions. The first guideline that I take from him, therefore, is simply that we cannot account for what happens in language—what we do with it and what it does to us—by recourse to other "sources" of one sort or another—cultural habits or social developments or psychological principles, and so on—as if these things were themselves somehow unlinguistic—foundations or exoskeletons forming language from beyond itself. For such "origins" are nothing if they are not themselves verbal; our very perception of them depends upon and is provided for by what we know how to say. "Grammar" for Wittgenstein "comes before facts."[1]

Wittgenstein's work may be seen to support, then, both an overriding concern with language itself and a descriptive rather than an explanatory method of enacting this concern. For if it seems, as it often does to me, that his arguments are irrefutable, that is because he usually gives nothing in the way of "explanation" to refute. He describes how we speak, and in so doing he shows that ultimately our speech is "ungrounded," that it makes no sense to ask why we do as we do; the varieties of verbal behavior can be delineated, and within themselves each may be intelligible in its own way, but our "whole language-game," the entire "grammar" within which we operate, is only the aggregation of these varieties of behavior, which are responsive in a multitude of ways both to themselves and to the actual situations where they may be applied. Attempts to "essentialize" this aggregation do nothing so much as reveal its lack of uniformity, while attempts to attribute its disparities to some imaginary, stable source fall back themselves into language. We can know how language functions from place to place and time to time, and those functions are all contained in the general grammar itself, which we can also invoke, as I shall demonstrate, in certain ways. But we should not, as Wittgenstein has it, say more than we know, nor confuse all the language that we can call up with that which we can actually and locally use.

"Swell advice," as Jake Barnes says in *The Sun Also Rises*: "Try and take it sometime. Try and take it." For, as I shall suggest more fully in a moment, one of the most important features of language that I shall be concerned with is the urgency within language of the motive to "say more than we know"; in conversations or in individual texts or even within language's entire history, this inclination to say more than *could* be "known" is not only our most dominating verbal interest but also generates the verbal forms we find most compelling. If Wittgenstein, as I have suggested, is concerned with the differences among all the various language-games that we play, he is also concerned with the philosophical necessity of marking one difference above all: the difference between verbal expressions that are meaningful and those that are not, the difference between the active and applied uses of words and the "mere" saying of them.

His first interest, again, was not in "literary" expression but in the nature of "ordinary," meaningful employments of language, and this is perhaps why some philosophers maintain that his investigations are irrelevant to literary studies. But I shall try to show that what in Wittgenstein's view so confuses philosophers about meaning in language is both a source of related confusions in literary criticism and also the source of the power of certain kinds of literary expression. When in Wittgenstein's accounts a philosopher holds up his hand in front of his face and declares, "This certainly is a hand," or when another stares fixedly at a tree and says, "That is a tree; I *know* that," both, I would claim, are engrossed by an "experience of words" in many of the same ways that we may be in reading literature, and both philosophers are just as mistaken as we are if we suppose that what engages us in these instances, what so compels and exercises our attention, is a matter of certain "knowledge" or "meaning." In this way, not only is philosophy as Wittgenstein practices it relevant to literary studies, but the forms of language that stimulate and obstruct that philosophy may be found, and perhaps best described, in literary process itself.

These fascinating and confusing verbal forms I shall call, for reasons that may later be clear, "grammatical displays." I now want to give a fuller description—though still a tentative one pending further demonstration—of what that concept means. Wittgenstein is primarily occupied, once again, with language's meaningful action, and his most fundamental argument is that it means in its "use." But a use of language for him is not a mere saying of words; it is an application of words to do something, an application that is both purposive and consequential. This application takes place, furthermore, on public ground and may be recognized and measured by "outward criteria." To the extent that they are meaningful, our "intentions" must be "embedded" in "situations," for example; and "obeying a rule" is not *thinking* that one is doing so, but consists in the actual and particular application of the rule; and our "mental experiences" of words—our attendant "associations," perhaps—are never necessarily relevant to or restrictive upon the meanings they constitute and accomplish, which depend upon communal institutions and practices. In all such meaningful usage—and this is a crucial point that I shall enlarge upon—it is the *action* of language that is important; in meaningful verbal activity, words themselves are relatively self-effacing in favor of the changes their uses achieve.

What Wittgenstein constantly struggles with and exposes, however, as he pursues these dynamics of meaningfulness in language, is a set of verbal conditions that may be seen as opposite to those that yield meaning. In these conditions, language is not doing any work; it is "idling." One's attention is drawn to it as language, and so it no longer functions as a foundation or vehicle or background for meaning, but is itself foregrounded and dominating. And it is here—with language in this relatively inactive and self-isolated condition—that the "mental" or "imaginative" *experience* of words comes into play, both as a philosophical problem and as the very substance of certain forms of literary expression.

This is language in its "grammatical" state, in which its effects are generated and governed not by local or particular application but only by a language-wide system of verbal possibilities. The "sense" that words may have—may even be felt to "possess"—under grammatical conditions is not tied down to specific uses and situations; words therefore communicate an awareness of "possible meanings," of the potential and capacity in language (and so in ourselves) for making meaning. Under these conditions our apprehension of words is more physical and substantial than it is in meaningful usage, since language does not disappear into action but takes all our attention, and this is one of the reasons why the perception of it may be felt as an "experience," as an actual "content." But at the same time this perception is flexible and multiple, and the words in view may attach to all sorts of actually remembered, lived situations. Thus, the displayed power of language generates the imagination of both past and potential experience, of capacity and capability, in the audience of its display.

Throughout his philosophical work after the *Tractatus*, Wittgenstein is most often concerned, once more, with "grammatical" expressions for the confusions they generate in seeming to be what they are not. They cannot be meaningful, for in their expression they are disconnected from any actual situations that would give them any particular meaning, that would render them, to put this another way, true or false. And yet the danger of language in this grammatical mode is that, precisely because of its evident independence from particular situations, it seems extraordinarily "sayable," apt, and immune from the criterial judgments to which words in particular applications are susceptible. It is therefore philosophically crucial to distinguish between grammatical expressions and those expressions that are meaningful, that provide information, function as descriptions, and apply to particular cases: "empirical propositions." In Wittgenstein's later philosophy, this discrimination depends largely, as I have suggested, upon the criterion of "use"; the easiest way to determine that an expression is a legitimate proposition is to ask if the language in it is being used to a purpose. But it is not only this later connection between meaning and use that both enables and requires the identification of grammatical expressions. Wittgenstein was assured of the possibility of this identification, in a less practical and more logical way, in the *Tractatus*.

To understand the usefulness of this earlier approach, and, more important, to appreciate the enormous force of the contrast between propositional and grammatical language, we might begin with an apparently commonsense distinction. Some expressions, we might say, are "about" the world, and describe our experience of it, and these are "empirical." But others, in one way or another, are statements about our language, and draw out or draw attention to its rules, and these are "grammatical." One trouble with this distinction, however, is that it presumes both a clarity of motive and process and a set of proportions that are not enacted in our general verbal behavior. For that behavior constantly features expressions that are in fact language-directed and language-oriented, even as if we were continually teaching language to each other, but which are offered as or seem indistinguishable from statements about the world, about our changing experience. This is most easily demonstrated by observing how frequently our remarks to each other take the form of definitions or redefinitions, or of logical—which is here to say, "grammatical"—extensions from them, while these remarks may seem to be further descriptions of "empirical" facts, or new information. It is only, perhaps, when we stop and examine such verbal gestures that we may see that they are not devoted to any particular case in question, that they do not advance whatever verbal sequence is in progress. Instead, and even though no "language teaching" would seem obviously legitimate in such instances, their appeal is not to temporary situational description. They draw attention to themselves *as expressions*, and in doing so take on a strangely substantial, nontemporary, and authoritative status. Even though they are not the implements of any recognized "teaching," they incline toward the character and force of a rule of expression because they seem to reach toward or even to exemplify such a rule, and thus they seem ways of access to principles or laws higher or more permanent than those that might govern more applied, active, and meaningful verbal sequences.

Perhaps more often than anything else in our verbal behavior, to put this another way, we speak as if we were "citing" language, and merely this can convert our expressions from one status to another and seem to give them a special and strange force. If such self-exposed, citational utterances were to occur in a classroom, of course, or in a philosophical discussion, then their relevance to the conceptual situation at hand would be measurable—which is another way of saying that they would function as propositions. But I am suggesting that we often speak this way to no such obvious pedagogical purpose, and that when we do, what we produce, rather than propositions of any sort, are undirected verbal displays, shows of signifying power that seem the richer precisely because they have no immediate relevance, and whose weight derives from the unlimited authority of grammar.

Part of the difficulty in distinguishing the grammatical from the empirical, the "idling" expression from the working one, then, resides in the frequency and force of the grammatical in our general linguistic behavior. For it seems natural to suppose that our most telling utterances are so because of their relation to our experience, to suppose that a "strong" remark must be so because it *is* "about" the world we observe. And even if on examination many of these utterances did seem more "about" words than the world, they might still seem to be descriptive of something; their very "aboutness" might seem a sign that they yielded information. So how is one to say where talk about the world ends and talk about words begins?

This problem traces back to a fundamental flaw in the commonsense distinction, which proposed that the difference between the grammatical and the empirical was to be defined by the "object" or the "material" toward which each mode of speech was directed. The very *assumption* that both are "directed," however—which follows inevitably from the seemingly harmless supposition that language's "aboutness" is reliably constant—blurs their difference; it implies that both verbal modes are meaningful because both are applied to some purpose. To suppose that these different sorts of expression are "about" something, in other words, begs the question of "use" and seems to render the criterion of "meaning as use" impotent for the discrimination between the grammatical and the meaningful.

We might therefore conclude either that there is not any decisive difference of the sort I have been claiming between grammatical and meaningful expression or that the concept of "meaning as use" is itself faulty. Neither inference, in my view, is ultimately warranted; there are arguments out of this predicament. But these arguments are quite complicated, and their complications might belie the sharpness of the distinction between "idling" and working language of which Wittgenstein seems convinced. Yet we may, again, approach this difference in another way by means of a measure that seems fundamentally unchanged throughout Wittgenstein's philosophic career: his discrimination between what can be *said* and what can be *shown*.

This distinction may itself seem puzzling, especially if one first encounters it, as I did, in Wittgenstein's later philosophy, where it is usually unexplained. But what it means is fully spelled out, I believe, in the *Tractatus* in Wittgenstein's treatment of the logical form of propositions. Here is Anthony Kenny's account of this effect of "showing" in language:

> The would-be propositions of philosophical logic, Wittgenstein thought, were attempts to *say* what was *shown* by the tautologies. The distinction between saying and showing was fundamental in both his earlier and his later philosophy. For instance, Wittgenstein wrote:
>
> > What expresses *itself* in language *we* cannot express by means of language.
> > Propositions *show* the logical form of reality.
> > They display it.
> > Thus, one proposition '*fa*' shows that the object *a* occurs in its sense, two propositions '*fa*' and '*ga*' show that the same object is mentioned in both of them . . .
> > What *can* be shown cannot be said.[2]

But later in Wittgenstein's thinking, as Kenny also observes, this "displaying" function of propositions was not supposed evident merely in the "tautologies" of logic, nor was the "logical form" of language itself so narrowly conceived. The latter concept expanded and articulated into Wittgenstein's conception of "logical grammar," or "logical syntax," and the "tautology" came to be considered as "only one way of displaying matters of syntax."[3] The "objects" so displayed, furthermore, are "real" not in any phenomenal sense but because they are "elements of the method of representation. . . . It is senseless to ask whether objects are more like substances or like properties or relations: objects belong to the method of representation . . ." (*W*, 110).

The density and ramifications of this argument may be difficult to comprehend easily in this short space, but they may be summarized, I think fairly, as follows: every proposition, even as it says what it says—as it describes a case, provides new information, generates meaning, and so on—also displays its *form* of doing so, its grammar, comprising both the "elements" and the "mode" of representation, and this grammar is the most fundamental property of our world.[4] Some expressions, such as tautologies, do nothing but function as such displays. They do not "say" anything. They do not describe, nor give information, nor apply to any particular case. And this means that they are not "about" anything at all, and that so to conceive them is fundamentally mistaken.[5] Rather, they confirm or reconfirm what the speakers of a language already "know," or presuppose in their verbal behavior, by exhibiting some part of the rules of their language. But this phenomenon of the exposure of linguistic form is not limited to such severely logical expressions. In the discussions to follow I shall extend Wittgenstein's conception by claiming that we may apprehend different balances or proportions of "saying" and "showing" from one expression to another, that some expressions seem to assert or describe so emphatically that our awareness of their grammatical form is inconsequential, while others, especially certain varieties of literary expression, do just the opposite and deemphasize and suppress their functions as meaningful sayings, and by that means generate an intense apprehension of grammatical possibility, of the logical necessities of language.

This distinction between utterances that "say" and those that "show" the forms of saying is the truest means of identifying what I am calling "grammatical expressions." But this test itself, once more, is only important because the seductive and deceptive power of these expressions—which is perceptible even in low-energy cases like tautologies—needs to be marked and distinguished from the process and effects of verbal "meaning." For these purposes the crucial inferences to be drawn from Wittgenstein—from a line of argument that runs, once again, from the *Tractatus* throughout his philosophic work—are, first, that certain verbal organizations may function to exhibit their mode of saying rather than to assert or propose anything, and, second, that what is exhibited in such instances is language's logical—or, more flexibly, grammatical—form. What is exposed is the very capacity for meaning, the potential and possibility of signification, and this is why these verbal forms are both so powerful and so mysterious.

The ways in which the logical form of language may be foregrounded, and in which its meaningful applications may be deemphasized, as I shall demonstrate in what follows, are various. But one further clarification must be made at this point: the grammatical aspects of expressions, which are quite different from their meanings and indeed become most evident when meaning is in abeyance, amount to the *sense* that they possess apart from their applications. Early in the *Notebooks 1914–1916*, Wittgenstein gives a sketch of two stick figures fencing and comments upon it as follows: "If the right-hand figure in this picture represents the man A, and the left-hand one stands for the man B, then the whole might assert, e.g. 'A is fencing with B.' The proposition in picture writing can be true and false. It has a sense independent of its truth and falsehood. It must be possible to demonstrate everything essential by considering this case."[6] "The proposition in picture writing can be true *and* false": it will be true *or* false depending upon the actual, real situation to which it is applied, or which it is held to "represent." But "it has a sense independent of its truth and falsehood." This "sense," then, is the capacity of the proposition for truth or falsehood, for meaningful application, but it is not itself a matter of meaning. And it is this sense that we may understand in propositions, whether they are brought to bear upon any actual case or not. This fundamental distinction between the isolated sense that a proposition may display in itself and the meaning that is generated only in the relation of the proposition to "reality" is crucial, both to Wittgenstein's thinking and to my purposes, for it explains not only how we understand unapplied, unmeaningful expressions but also *what* we understand in them, and what it is that "grammatical expressions" show rather than say.

These expressions that have sense but not meaning, these "grammatical displays," thus seem to contain the possibilities of meaning because they express not what applies to any particular situation or purpose but what might apply to any number of situations; the coherence of such language, and its sanction, has nothing to do with specific conditions but is founded, merely, upon the grammatical conformations shown in it. Grammatical expressions thus possess both the arbitrariness and the certainty of language involved only with itself. They seem truer than any more applied language—though of course they are no more true than they are false—because they are detached from any local developments that might verify or contradict them. They are beyond truth.

Although such grammatical exhibitions make up a large part of our everyday verbal behavior, they are most remarkable and powerful in certain forms of literary expression. Indeed, it is the revelation of grammatical capacity that may be seen to generate the power of these expressions; for when extended verbal sequences take on "grammatical" status, they may be recognized, as I shall demonstrate at some length, as alternative and integral languages in their own right, with all the signifying capacity that such recognition acknowledges, and a reader's response to them will then be both willing and versatile.

In some ways this disposition to grant language unrestricted power when it is presented as a language is the same as an attitude in the original learning of language as Maurice Merleau-Ponty describes it. He suggests, in *Consciousness and the Acquisition of Language*, that we are mistaken if we think that such learning involves an aggressively assertive effort, as if to translate what one heard into some already known protolanguage. This amounts to a misconception of the action and role of the self in the process, which should be figured not so much as an inherent intelligibility trying to assert itself but as a more undetermined and receptive disposition to an imposing and articulated linguistic establishment. This is not to deny egoistic motivation, or individual ambition, in such cases but to reverse the form which that ambition is usually imagined to take: to see it as an effort to fit the self to the language rather than vice versa. One "masters" a language not by conquering it, but by infiltrating it, inhabiting it.

But this has to do with an original learning of language. And one obvious difference between that and the kind of case into which I am inquiring is that in the latter there is much more to the "self"; we are already in full possession of various languages prior to encountering a new one. If, therefore, we find ourselves responding as receptively to a text as if we were learning a language, then we must somehow have been moved to relax our hold on what we know in favor of what we do not. But the examples I shall describe, and our probable responses to them, will, I think, account for such a relaxation, for we shall see in them how the presence of language as such is reciprocal with the perception that something "original" is happening. When language's meaningful functioning is suspended, when the *possibilities* of meaning hold sway, the imaginative situation seems renewed, and new knowledge, new uses, seem imminent. Perhaps this is because we have learned the trick of such situations, and the very fact of knowing many useful vocabularies increases our receptiveness to a possible new one and inclines us to think that any verbal set that is disconnected from use might be, eventually, turned to it. More likely, it is because the more uses for certain words that we know, then the more powerful will be a display of those words that suspends those uses, the greater the expectation of some meaning beyond our present capacity. However else we might explain the matter, it would seem that grammatical exhibitions appear original to us in proportion to the number and complexity of working vocabularies that they appear to set aside.

For these and other reasons, grammatical displays are so engaging that they appear to be one sort of thing we live for. They may generate, as I have suggested, a powerful illusion of capability. Or they may present us with a real "grammatical" capability that, if we try to use it, to apply it more locally and particularly, most often dissolves as an illusion, though usually not without causing some trouble where we thought it would work. When extended beyond aesthetic contexts, for example—by which here I mean merely contexts of verbal "play," obviously "fictional" contexts—the confidence generated by grammatical displays may become very dangerous indeed. Probably it is what stimulated Plato to throw out the poets.

When we perceive language "as such," therefore, language isolated from and more forceful than any use of it, we should also recognize that it cannot be turned to any immediate use. This is to say that because it is not "interpretable" in any single direction, because it seems irreplaceable and untranslatable, it cannot be used. Thus, to be aware of language's presence and potential in the ways I am considering is not, at that moment, to "understand" anything in the ordinary, workable sense of that term. In Wittgenstein's conception, once again, language in this condition is "idling," though one would want to add here that when the revolutions per minute get as high as they can in some literary expressions, "idling" is no longer the right word for verbal forms whose inertia—their resistance to singular employments—is enormous but whose activity within themselves—in the integral and complex play of their exposed possibilities—is very quick indeed.

It is this meaningless and inapplicable power that makes the "experience of language" an *experience*, whereas the functional working of active words cannot be said, by Wittgenstein's measure, ever necessarily to involve "experience" at all. Where meaning is concerned, it is the imagination that is "idle," and meaning itself is an action that is not perceptible or definable as a feeling or conceivable as any other sort of what one might call "experience content." But grammatical exhibitions do seem to hold or to carry a "content" and inevitably to engender some of the kinds of perception we call "experience," here indissociable from the life of the language itself.

We should not suppose, however, that this experience of language is to be explained by what are called in psychology "associations." It is true that in "grammatical exhibitions" the normal *accompaniments* of meaning—certain feelings for certain words, for example—are foregrounded with the words they attach to. And it is equally true that our perceptions in these cases involve imaginative "experiences" that seem deeply personal, but these are neither necessarily secret or hidden, nor are they restricted or determined only by one's individual history.[7] For it is not so much what particular "associations" we have for the words of a text that matters—since one could never insist on the exclusive relevance of his associations as opposed to someone else's—but that the imaginative act of *having* associations is built in, or evidently called for, by "grammatical displays." Evidently we should say that it is *possible* associations, like possible meanings, that are in question here—since one does not have to remember them to imagine having them—and that the activeness or substantialness of such possible feelings for language is yet another result of the suppression of meaning.

Of course, our feelings of and for words are not public in the way that meanings may be, nor can we communicate them as we can meanings, for we can never be sure, as Wittgenstein says, if other people "have this experience too" (*PI*, p. 181). Nonetheless, we learn such feelings as we learn language; and we have continual evidence that they are experienced—whatever their specific qualities may be—by other people. In this way they may be said to be part of language, properties of language that are more vitally exposed when language is "idling." I would propose, then, that in grammatical exhibitions it is the associative *capacity* of words that comes intensely into play and invites those personal responses that neither restrict nor exhaust their source.

It is one of the signs of the power of this "associativeness" of language in its grammatical condition that we characteristically adopt toward it a double and paradoxical attitude: we think of it, again, as secret, hidden, and personal to ourselves, but at the same time we think of it as the truest sort, or the realest sort, of "meaning." This is the attitude, I believe, that is reflected in our cultural interest in or appetite for certain features of Freudian psychology, for example, and specifically for Freud's proposition—in *The Psychopathology of Everyday Life* (1901) and in the *Introductory Lectures to Psychoanalysis* (1916–17)—that certain sorts of grammatical accidents are *meaningful*, his conception that slips of the tongue and other parapraxes ("faulty acts" or "faulty functions") are revealing of unconscious thoughts and purposes, and hence of meanings, that are more real or significant than conscious ones. I have suggested elsewhere that Freud has a great deal of trouble justifying logically the existence of the "unconscious," not only because he conceives it as a source for motives and behavior that we are accustomed to think of as "conscious"—since these involve rapid editing and rewriting of our speech, for example, as well as all sorts of elaborate plotting and scheming—but also because he himself must paradoxically describe this unconscious with the vocabulary of consciousness.[8] Wittgenstein has characterized the trouble here precisely.

> The idea of there being unconscious thoughts has revolted many people. Others again have said that these were wrong in supposing that there could only be conscious thoughts, and that psychoanalysts had discovered unconscious ones. The objectors to unconscious thought did not see that they were not objecting to the newly discovered psychological reactions, but to the way in which they

> were described. The psychoanalysts on the other hand were misled by their own way of expression into thinking that they had done more than discover new psychological reactions; that they had, in a sense, discovered conscious thoughts which were unconscious. (BB, 57)

And it should be clear from this excerpt that Wittgenstein is not claiming that there is no "unconscious," no such "psychological reactions" that might be so designated. Nor am I making such a claim. For it is not Freud's postulation of unconscious processes that seems wrong, but his insistence that these processes are secretly similar to and continuous with conscious ones, and that both of them must work to produce singularly interpretable results. What I want to propose instead, which may be obvious from what I have already suggested about the operation of "grammatical" motives and effects in human speech, is that a slip of the tongue, for example—a remark inappropriate to or nonsensical in an otherwise meaningful verbal sequence—amounts to an eruption into that sequence, whether more or less "accidental," of general grammatical possibility, from which we are made momentarily aware of what else might have been said, said often in "opposition," to the immediate and actual purposes of the sequence in question.

Now any display of grammatical possibility, as I have begun to show, may be very powerful for us. It reveals to us our capacity for all manner of speech; it generates an illusion of imaginative freedom; and it gives us to suppose that we *could* "mean" anything we liked. For all these motives and more, therefore, it will be tempting to take such displays as actual meanings, or rather as meanings more real than any actual ones we might ordinarily accomplish. This is because grammatical possibility, once more, is in its peculiar way indeed more "real" or "certain" than any locally and temporarily defined significance. In the case of the latter, one may be mistaken, and what one says may be proved false; whereas in the "grammatical," so long as one makes *some* sort of sense, neither mistakes nor truth are in question.

It is this characteristic strength and independence of grammatical expressions, I would argue, that italicizes them when they occur as slips or accidents, that makes them seem to invite greater attention than the sequences they interrupt, and gives us to attribute to them some sort of meaning beyond meaning. The difficulty with such a response is that these accidental grammatical displays are evidently not, by ordinary criteria, meaningful at all; they do not possess the characteristics of meaning, the most crucial of which here is a singularly purposive application as opposed to an undetermined multiplicity of implication and association. How, then, could their "grammatical" condition ever be seriously or finally mistaken for that of meaning? How can what occurs as complex verbal possibility be ostensibly restricted to some single and telling sense?

Freud tries to accomplish such a conversion by recourse to verbal situations that he presumes—and I shall say more about this presumption in a moment—can be regarded as sources of language that is *both* "accidental" and "meaningful." The examples of revelatory slips of the tongue in which he has most confidence, and to which he most frequently appeals, are taken from imaginative literature, and more specifically from the speeches and actions of characters in novels, poems, and plays. And what such examples appear to provide him with, more than anything else, are apparently human situations in which there is a guaranteed hierarchy of "knowledge." A "literary" situation, in this view, is authored, and its author is one who knows something, and knows it best. His audience, for its part, wants to know what the author knows, wants to discover, that is, what is already known and determined. What both author and audience know about, furthermore, are characters who are presumed ignorant.

Of course, we may not usually suppose that most literary expression lays itself out in this way—as a source of meanings so determined as to amount to matters of "knowledge." I have already suggested—and shall continue to show—that the dramatization or display of "possible meanings" in various literary forms is not the same as meaning itself, and that therefore the response appropriate to it is not any reductively "interpretive" act that might result in the sort of knowledge Freud wants. What one "knows" about in these "grammatical exhibitions," once more, is that expressions or gestures are complex and potential. It is not *what* the man who habitually deposits his ten-bladed pocket knife in the ladies' laps is doing, but all that he *might* be doing—all this gesture might mean—that we "understand." The "knowledge" supplied by even the rather simple literary examples that Freud fancies is not of some singular solution to a puzzle but of an irreducible set of possibilities. Thus, we may consider that a good deal of violence has to be done to them in order to transform them into one-way streets to someone's "knowledge" about someone else. But this sort of transformation is invaluable for Freud because when a literary situation is perceived in this way, it corresponds to a clinical one; the ignorant or mistaken character becomes analogous to the neurotic patient who submits himself to one who knows or will know his case better than he himself does, and, like a knowing audience, will discover in it a meaning that was unknown to the subject but nonetheless present and predetermined, as if by an author, in the form of a "mental illness." Of course, the great majority of the cases under Freud's scrutiny in his discussions of parapraxes in the *Introductory Lectures* and in *The Psychopathology of Everyday Life*, as the title of the second work indicates, are not clinical ones; they are "normal" incidents of apparently accidental behavior to which Freud wants to attribute the same sort of ground rules that he could presume in cases of admitted neurotic disease. This is why the "literary" examples that he gathers are so important to him. They avail him—at least given the determined spectacles through which he sees them—of a pattern identical to the clinical model but evidently more legitimately applicable to human behavior at large. And his grounds for such application is simply his own conviction that human life is just as patently significant as life on a stage in his peculiar view of it. If someone supposes that parapraxes are "just small chance events," Freud declares: "What does the fellow mean by this? Is he maintaining that there are occurrences, however small, which drop out of the universal concatenation of events—occurrences which might just as well not happen as happen? If anyone makes a breach of this kind in the determinism of natural events at a single point, it means that he has thrown overboard the whole *Weltanshauung* of science" (IL, 28).

Whether we find such an attitude ridiculous or irritating or embarrassing, we shall not be surprised to discover that the "cases" that support it have been very violently revised indeed; they are so determined and pat that they seem fantastic. There is the story of the waiter who, after announcing that the price of a dish had been increased by a certain amount but not so noted on the menu, fumbled with the money he was given and dropped a coin of just that amount back on the table—thus demonstrating his dishonesty and remorse at the same time. Or of the woman who forgot to try on her wedding dress on the eve of the wedding, and soon after the ceremony was divorced. Or of the married woman who "frequently signed documents in her maiden name" and was subsequently divorced. Or of others "who have lost their wedding-rings during the honeymoon, and I know too that the history of their marriages has given a sense to the accident.—And now here is one more glaring example, but with a happier ending. The story is told of a famous German chemist that his marriage did not take place, because he forgot the hour of his wedding and went to the laboratory instead of to the church. He was wise enough to be satisfied with a single attempt and died at a great age unmarried" (IL, 58).

Such examples are indeed glaring, of course, but not for the reason that Freud supposes. The truth is that one is hard put to find even in literature plots so neat or characters so mechanical and predictable as these. Such prescribed behavior, such lip-smackingly inevitable outcomes, are rare—except perhaps in Poe, or in certain children's stories. And like such stories, Freud's examples to show that "faulty actions" have a "sense" always read from back to front. Hindsight is indispensable to their form; it is what reduces grammatical possibility to something that Freud can figure as an actual, realized meaning. He tells of the officer who while riding in a horse race with his fellows fell and was fatally injured. Before the race "he had been deeply depressed by the death of his beloved mother, had had fits of sobbing in the company of his fellow officers, and to his trusted friends had spoken of being weary of life. . . . Finally, before the race . . . he expressed gloomy forebodings; with the view that we hold in these matters, it will not remain a surprise to us that these forebodings turned out to be justified" (PEL, 182). But neither would it have surprised us, who may not hold such a view, if they had not, all depending on what ultimately happened to the officer. So many of Freud's examples resemble certain detective shows on television, such as *Columbo*, in which the crime is committed at the beginning, in the audience's sight, so that the detective's positively clairvoyant reading of the clues—his restriction of the possibilities—seems utterly natural. Knowing what happened, knowing what will happen, is a foolproof angle from which to convert the multiple implications of a set of expressions to a singular meaning, and this conversion can be so impressive that one may forget—as Freud constantly does—that these expressions can only be read as a meaningful *sequence* because their structural possibilities were never really possible, because their eventual restriction was preordained.

Here again we may see that the logical problem of Freud's arguments concerning slips of the tongue and the like—in which "unconscious" processes are unsatisfactorily distinguished from conscious ones—goes very deep. For it bespeaks his own actual unrecognition of the unconscious itself. There is nothing free or wild or irrational about the unconscious—attributes that Freud will claim for it elsewhere—in its function in Freud's "literary" cases. It traffics in the same sort of meanings and purposes as do the conscious operations it sometimes interrupts and replaces. It is not revelatory of associative possibilities, but rather of "meaningful" chains more determined and foregone—and, of course, more boring—than anything the conscious mind has ordinarily to offer.

It should be noted again that I am not proposing that the "unconscious" does not exist, but only that the modeling of it upon processes and motives that are if anything hypermeaningful is nonsense. More important, I am certainly not objecting to the notion that an "unconscious" might be composed of *some* sort of language. Rather, I would suggest, once again, that "accidents" in speech are the results of our assimilation of and perpetual access to the grammatical possibilities of our language. This is a recognition that some of Freud's revisionists—most notably Jacques Lacan—sometimes seem to approach.

Lacan considers, for instance, that phrases like Freud's "unconscious thought" are *not* contradictory precisely because "the unconscious participates in the functions of ideation, even of thought" (*SLP*, 20), and it does so just because it is itself composed of language—as if the unconscious might be figured as the entire learned totality of the possibilities of language—which I have called the "grammar"—unrestricted by any immediate and particular applications or intentions. Here one may be so gratified to discover that the importance of such grammatical possibility is acknowledged by a psychologist that Lacan's formulation may become too eagerly accepted. But we should proceed with caution here, for this agreeable assumption of "the omnipresence of human discourse"—in which even the unconscious mind should be considered as somehow "structured like a language"—often reveals itself as a much more restrictive conception where language is not present as a system of possibilities but working, even unconsciously, as a secret but quite meaningful code. A "subject" is introduced by the analyst into a "*primary Language* in which, beyond what he tells us of himself, he is already talking to us unbeknownst to him" (*SLP*, 57; Lacan's emphasis).

This conception of "unconscious language" as a source of meanings and knowledge to which only psychoanalysts are privy may be indistinguishable from Freud's own. The powerful influences and effects of the body of language, of the grammar, within our speaking behavior that I am describing are neither so occult as this nor, when discovered, so revelatory, exactly because they are merely a matter of language's complex and variegated texture, of its surface of possibility as we learn it. And if they seem magical—or "significant" beyond anything we might say in a meaningful way—this is not because they are varieties of some sort of hypermeaning, but because they are not meanings at all; rather, they are signs of our very *capability* of, and of our language's *potential* for, meaningful expression, exhibitions of verbal power and freedom that in fact can never be realized since they *are* meaningful only in restrictive applications, when we know what we must say, or when the mystery has already been solved.

I have tried to suggest that this is a discrimination that Freud willfully ignores not in order to single out his conceptions or our interest in them as perversely misguided, but to show that these conceptions and this interest are indicative of a fundamental and natural problem within our verbal behavior and of the self-contradictory lengths to which we may go in order to solve it. The difficulty, once more, is in our inclination to imagine our experience of language, to imagine our feelings for words, as matters of meaning, and to justify that imagining by supposing that grammatical possibilities both originate and are turned to meaningful purposes in the mind. But these possibilities—whether they end up, as everything usually does, "in the mind" or not—would not be so fascinating to us, I think, if they were originally "mental," if they were not perceived within our most substantial and direct apprehension of language itself, and if it were not so hard for us to conceive that something so vital to ourselves could be a matter of grammar.

This confusion of the perception of the features of grammar with the realization of meaning, especially the sort of "meaning" that must be located "in the mind," occurs throughout literary studies, but nowhere is it more evident than when we try to describe literary expression most immediately and directly in the process that we call close reading. I now want to look at the best close reader that I have seen, but not merely to show how deeply and compellingly "grammatical displays" may be taken for matters of meaning, and certainly not to try to invalidate William Empson's reading itself. What I want to consider is how our reception of his readings, so many of them brilliant, has suffered from the confusion of grammatical perceptions with something either "meaningful" or "personal" or both, how this confusion not only puzzles Empson in his own justifications for what he is doing but also has allowed many to discount his work as an exercising of ingenious but idiosyncratic opinions.

I could not, even if it were my intention, demonstrate in this space just how ingenious Empson's reading consistently is; I shall have to refer largely, without examples, to the richness of his reading practice so as to suggest that its appeal to the grammatical features of language is neither dismissable as an expression of a merely personal bent nor justifiable, even by Empson himself, as a matter of "meaning." In the following excerpt, he cites a speech of Macbeth's, "when he is spurring on his jaded hatred to the murder of Banquo and Fleance," and he concentrates on the line, "Light thickens, and the Crow/Makes Wing to th' Rookie Wood."

> Come, seeling Night
> Skarfe up the tender Eye of Pitiful Day
> And with thy bloddie and invisible Hand

Cancel and teare to pieces that great Bond
That keeps me pale.
Light thickens, and the Crow
Makes Wing to th' Rookie Wood.
Good things of Day begin to droope, and drowse,
While Night's black Agents to their Prey's does rowse.
Thou marvell'st at my words, but hold thee still;
Things bad begun, make strong themselves by ill:
So prythee go with me.

(III. ll. 50.)

The condition of his skin (By the pricking of my thumbs, / Something wicked this way comes), the sense of being withdrawn far within his own flesh (like an old lecher, a small fire at his heart, all the rest on's body cold), the sense that the affair is prosaic, it need not be mentioned, and yet an occasional squawking of the nerves (Hobbidance croaks in Tom's belly), in short the whole frame of body, as I read the lines, is lit up and imposed upon the reader, from which Macbeth lashes his exhausted energies into a new, into the accustomed, readiness for murder.

I have tried by these almost irrelevant quotations to show how much work the reader of Shakespeare is prepared to do for him, how one is helped by the rest of his work to put a great deal into any part of it, but this seems to explain very little. Various similar sound effects or associations may be noted; there is a suggestion of witches' broth, or curdling blood, about *thickens*, with the vowel sound of *light*, coming next to it, with the movement of stirring treacle, and the cluck of the k-sounds, intensifying a suggestion, too, of harsh, limpid echo, and, under careful feet of poachers, an abrupt crackling of sticks. The vowel sounds at the end make an increasing darkness as the *crow* goes forward. But, after all, one would be very surprised if two people got the same result from putting a sound-effect into words in this way.

It is safer to point out that *rooks* were, in any case, creatures of foreboding . . . . (*STA*, 18–21)

One *would* be surprised if another person "got the same result from putting a sound-effect into words in this way," but it should be clear that, precisely because of the nature of sound effects, that does not for a moment invalidate Empson's characterization of this one, though we should not suppose, as perhaps we traditionally do, that this is because sound effects are restrictively "personal." And his apology that all the quotations from Shakespeare that he brings to bear on this moment may be "almost irrelevant" may seem itself irrelevant, because we may accept these associations as quite legitimate connections, since they constitute the obvious application of Shakespeare to Shakespeare. These are signs—as I shall show more fully in a moment—that Empson's gaze, as he reads this passage from Shakespeare, is outward rather than inward, that it is rather a matter of observation than of testimony. Though at this point we may be willing only to say that what makes his analysis seem impersonal, seem to have more to do with what is outside himself than inside, is the simple fact that his concentration upon the text that calls forth his thoughts never seems to waver.

Even so, our feeling that there is something intensely "personal" about Empson's reading, about his expressed "associations," may persist, just because these associations, however apt they may seem, are frequently amazing. Consider, for instance, the "suggestion" that he notes, in the "cluck of the k-sounds," of "harsh, limpid echo, and, under careful feet of poachers, an abrupt crackling of sticks." No one else, I would wager, could ever have had or articulated such a response without Empson's help—though many, having taken this cue, may now do so—and thus its apparent "rightness," as if it were something we might have expected, may set us wondering about why then we did not have it ourselves. Now many of the ways of answering this question are liable to be mistaken; and what we need to recognize here, I think, is that the aptness and the surprise of Empson's connections are not mutually exclusive because these connections are grammatical. This seems obviously true as one sees that Empson meets Shakespeare's grammatical displays with others of his own—rather than with more discursive summaries or interpretations—with turns of speech whose metaphoric disjunctiveness identifies them as such, and whose vocabulary and syntax often seem a match for Shakespeare's own. And the most important quality of this "grammaticalness" of Empson's readings is that their property seems public rather than private. They may be indeed surprising, but not because he has invented them; he seems rather to have discovered them, found things that we too might have found had we searched for them with his concentration and range of grammatical contacts.

This "outwardness" of Empson's vision is not only something continually observable in his critical practice, but it is something that he himself seems to presume. Even while he often apologizes for his individual license in bringing out such associations, he supposes as well that they are in fact properties of a text itself, and considers them implanted there by an author even when that author only seems to have "discovered" them himself in the act of writing: "An ambiguity of the fifth type occurs when the author is discovering his idea in the act of writing, or not holding it all in his mind at once, so that, for instance, there is a simile which applies to nothing exactly, but lies half-way between two things when the author is moving from one to the other. Shakespeare continually does it . . ." (*STA*, 155). He continues by supporting this observation with a passage from *Measure for Measure*, and then he remarks that "Ford is fond of the same device, possibly from imitation." But Empson's initial concern here with authors' minds, in the inference that they may sometimes not know what they are doing, does not compromise his assuredness that the possibilities of meaning in the text indeed constitute a "doing" not only that Shakespeare accomplishes "continually" but also that Ford could have imitated. And again we may see that the consistency that Empson is apprehending here, and with which he is working, is not an interior matter of "mind" at all.

The same conclusion may be reached when he justifies his associative reach to one set of limits or another by alluding to how a text is "meant," and even by identifying that text with a certain "order of mind." Despite the apparent "mentalness" of this sort of vocabulary, there is nothing personally "intentional" about Empson's defenses of his judgments. His frequent observations about how a phrase or line is "meant," or is "supposed to be taken," never trace to any author's predetermined "meaning," but are estimations of the relation between the expressed text and general grammatical possibility, and "orders of mind" are thus in fact orders of language. His interest in authorial intentions, like his fondness for alluding to the mental or emotional conditions of the writers he considers, seems motivated not by a desire to understand some restrictive plan and use it to "interpret" the work but by the impulse to apprehend more immediately the action of the writing itself. His personal and even psychological characterizations of authors, in this way, usually if not always seem to be allegories for expressing the vitality of his encounters with their complex expressions: "Milton is extremely cool about the matter; one is made to sit with him pleasantly in the shade, all day long, needing no further satisfaction; it is delightfully soothing to feel that the devil is all the time falling faster and faster" (*STA*, 12).

Therefore it seems—in the cases I have referred to and in many, many others—that Empson is employing some critical and theoretical concepts—and often "mental" ones—that were in his time traditional and current, and still are, but that do not accurately match or explain what he is doing in his reading. This is indicated not merely by his constant appeals to what I must conceive, once more, as matters not of some "mental meaning" but of grammatical possibility, and not merely by his occasional notice of something like a grammar most actively displaying itself: "A sort of unity may be given by the knowledge of a scheme on which all the [various, disjunctive] things occur; so that the scheme itself becomes the one thing being considered" (*STA*, 234). For this inference that the "knowledge" Empson himself exhibits and practices so acutely is a knowledge of something other than "mind" may also be drawn from his own expressed awareness of a sometimes missing connection within his own methods: "I have continually employed a method of analysis which jumps the gap between two ways of thinking; which produces a possible set of alternative meanings with some ingenuity, and then says it is grasped in the preconsciousness of the reader by a native effort of the mind" (*STA*, 239). But as he continues, we soon see that this "gap" need not be one, for this "native effort of the mind" as he subsequently describes it is not something that is prior to or beyond language. It is made possible, indeed, by a knowledge of language, for the "preconscious" is full of words: "Normal sensibility is a tissue of what has been conscious theory made habitual and returned to the pre-conscious" (*STA*, 254). What is "native" to the mind is the same as what has become "habitual" for it, and the "preconscious" for Empson is imagined as the historical product of previously articulated and assimilated verbal forms. So that the difference between "preconscious" and "conscious" apprehensions in reading is not between mysteriously unverbal mental conditions and evidently verbal ones, but between two very different modes of language. It may be that in Empson's conception these modes are not different enough, for I would hold that what is grasped here is not, again, a "set of alternative meanings" but a set of grammatical possibilities. Still, his conception of the "preconscious" seems much closer to what Lacan's idea of the unconscious—and Freud's before him—*ought* to have been: something not only produced by learning language but also—at least in my terms—constituted by language in its possible, implicative, and "grammatical" condition. Indeed, it seems to me not too much to propose that Empson, perhaps without fully realizing it and impeded by certain inherited concepts that were inadequate to his apprehension of literary expressions, virtually discovered in literature the importance of "grammar" in the sense that I have extended from Wittgenstein.

This is all I want to say by way of introduction about the force in our experience of "grammatical exhibitions" and the ramifications of this concept in literary studies. In the discussions that follow, I shall try to show how some different varieties of literary expression may be more fruitfully described as linguistic displays than measured upon a grid of meaning, and how our conceptions of more general literary processes—such as those of metaphor, for example—are especially illuminated if we see them as ways of access to grammatical possibility in which the action of a text opens up our language to us.

In the first chapter the fundamental and opposed conceptions of "meaning" as the applied use of words on the one hand and the "experience" of language through grammatical display on the other will be more patiently—or at least more slowly—defined with reference to Wittgenstein's insistence upon "outward criteria" for meaning and, especially, to his remarkable description of the "seeing of aspects" as a way into this concept of "grammatical experience." Then, in Language

As Such, I shall describe how certain sorts of verbal construction—a few among the many that are employed in literature to this effect—inevitably generate the perception of language exposed not merely as language but as *a* language, as an integral grammatical set that compels not assertive interpretation or analysis but acknowledgment. Forms of Voice is an effort to show how the sounded rhythms of speech may themselves constitute grammatical experiences and be perceived as ways of access to language's vitality rather than as catalysts, as traditionally they have been taken, for any supposedly more important signifying process. "Voice" in literary expression, I shall suggest, may range from the locally recognizable and colloquial form that we encounter most often in Robert Frost to the much less personally dramatic and more general "poetically" sounded form that we encounter in Wallace Stevens, but in both cases it generates experiences that trace to different ends of a *grammatical* spectrum.

"Grammatical perception" itself—as I shall maintain in the chapter on metaphor—is fundamentally indigenous to and perhaps most easily and obviously achieved in the verbal disjunctions and disparities of figurative usage, whose "unity" is founded not upon knowledge or meaning or any such conceptual bases but on the potential for "sense" that springs just from our awareness that in metaphors we are dealing expressly with language displayed—whose "coherence" may even derive simply from our recognition of a language as a syntax. And in Saying and Imagining, I am trying to see what may be inferred by reversing the traditional priority of those two concepts and by considering—as seems more descriptively accurate—that our capacity to "say" goes far beyond our capacity to "imagine" in the sense of "visualizing." "Imagining" is figured here as something we can do only with "local grammars," with vocabularies for which we can conceive actual and particular applications, so that our ability to see with the mind's eye is restricted to only a part, a fraction, of all our various ways of talking. From this it follows that the power of many sorts of expression—from the strange, unseeable "images" of certain poetry to the "forced imagining" and grammatical jokes of cartoons—is a function of the difference we perceive between merely verbal coherence and visually imaginable form.

Through all these accounts I shall continue to make use of Wittgenstein's philosophy, especially his invaluable discussions of meaning and "working language" and his remarks more specifically about "idling" grammatical expression. I am of course aware that I am extending the sense and relevance of the concept of "grammar" well beyond what he explicitly provides for, and I can only hope that readers will consider such extension justifiable and useful. But philosophy as Wittgenstein regards it is involved here, as I suggested earlier, in another way. For in our literary reading—both of the authors I discuss and many others—we are enmeshed, whether pleasurably or anxiously, in a philosophical predicament in which the multiple and possible meanings, the *sense* of grammatical forms, are in constant relation and tension with meanings we can actually make and apply. It may seem strange to say that literature has a "subject," or that philosophy has a "substance"—since the opposite alignments would seem more probable—but insofar as both can be said, grammar is the subject and the substance of both literature and philosophy. If in philosophy, as Wittgenstein practices it, we must recognize and avoid purely grammatical expression for the sake of clarity of meaning, in literature we are invited to this recognition as evidence of how much more than meaning there is to our experience of words. In either case, it is the grammar we shall have in sight.

CHAPTER ONE

Uses and Aspects: Meaning and the Experience of Words

> Don't all *experiences* of understanding get covered up by the use, by the *practice* of the language-game? And that merely means: here such experiences aren't of the slightest interest to us. (RPP 1: 184)

> If now the situation is that, while there *is* such a thing as an experience of meaning, this after all is something incidental, how in that case can it seem so very important? (RPP 1: 1050)

> Asked "Did you recognize your desk when you entered your room this morning?"—I should no doubt say "Certainly!" And yet it would be misleading to say that an act of recognition had taken place. Of course the desk was not strange to me; I was not surprised to see it, as I should have been if another one had been standing there, or some unfamiliar kind of object.
>
> No one will say that every time I enter my room, my long-familiar surroundings, there is enacted a recognition of all that I see and have seen hundreds of times before.
>
> It is easy to have a false picture of the processes called "recognizing"; as if recognizing always consisted in comparing two impressions with one another. . . . (PI, 602–4)

Of course, such concepts as "recognizing" sometimes must signify some sort of "mental" act, for that role is what provides the contrast here for those that do not, and from Wittgenstein's next paragraph we may begin to infer what the conditions of such acts might be: "We say 'The expression in his voice was *genuine*.' If it was spurious we think as it were of another one behind it.—*This* is the face he shews the world, inwardly he has another one.—But this does not mean that when his expression is *genuine* he has two the same" (PI, 606). The differentiation that Wittgenstein is working for here seems, for one thing, to be between perceiving "sameness" and perceiving "difference" in relation to the same object. Because seeing something as different from what it was or might have been may seem to involve two images, and hence a sort of mental doubleness, we may tend to suppose that seeing something as the same as it was—"recognizing" it for what it has always been—requires a similar process of matching or comparing, some relation or superimposition of separate images. But what Wittgenstein maintains is that seeing "sameness"—or "identity"—at least in certain cases, is fundamentally unlike seeing difference, that—in these cases—the former is a singular rather than a multiple dynamic, and hence it does not lend itself to description as a "mental activity."

But again, "recognizing," as well as a number of other such "mental" concepts, quite evidently has another sort of use in which it would describe an act of mind. Indeed, we seem most to favor this use for these sorts of concepts, so much so that we tend to presume it even when no such activity seems necessarily present. Terms like "thinking," "understanding," and the like seem tilted toward the description of "mental processes." And even Wittgenstein's most convincing demonstration that these terms do not have that sort of application, and that "mental processes" are not relevant in "ordinary" linguistic behavior—even his demonstration that the *meaning* of that behavior is not defined by reference to "mental" acts—occurs against a background of cases in which mental activity seems just what is in question. His excursions into this background will prove of immense value to literary description and its problems. The relatively simple idea here that in the perception of differences—differences within a single "object"—the "mind" is "active" in a way that it is not in more accustomed behavior may be connected to the conception that language itself is most active as language—and the mind similarly active in response to it—when it is not working in ordinary ways, and to a distinction between those complex verbal processes and perceptions that seem to stimulate immediate and correspondent *experiences* and those uses of language that do not. This is a distinction, I shall argue, that may be said even to define certain varieties of literary expression and response.

The categorical difference within language's general operation that I have just outlined is not something with which Wittgenstein begins in *Philosophical Investigations*, although later he will address himself to it expressly in many ways. In the earlier stages of *Philosophical Investigations* he is intent upon what is perhaps his most consistent philosophic concern: to mark the differences that may distinguish numerous, various, particular verbal processes from each other, especially when misleading analogies have obscured these differences and thus caused philosophical confusion. And his own larger or more synthetic analogues for language's overall condition are therefore, at the outset, disintegrative rather than otherwise: "Our language can be seen as an ancient city: a maze of little streets and squares, of old and new houses, and of houses with additions from various periods; and this surrounded by a multitude of new boroughs with straight regular streets and uniform houses" (PI, 18).

Even the two more determined models for language's action that he offers early in *Philosophical Investigations*, which will later appear both fundamental to his own thinking and important to linguistic philosophy more generally, are more differentiating than unifying. The first one is of language as a "tool": "Think of the tools in a tool-box: there is a hammer, pliers, a saw, a screw-driver, a rule, a glue-pot, glue, nails and screws.—The functions of words are as diverse as the functions of these objects" (PI, 11). It is especially this *diversity* of the tool model for language, and the flexibility of its implications, that allows one of Wittgenstein's most important and general philosophical assertions: "For a *large* class of cases—though not for all—in which we employ the word 'meaning' it can be defined thus: the meaning of a word is its use in the language" (PI, 43).

But the same "diversity" that makes this proposition accurate in a general way may make it seem, to a reader, little enough to say. Meaning is not always and everywhere "use," after all, but only in "a large class of cases," and "use in the language," itself, we might suppose, could be all sorts of things, even the mere pronouncing of a word in some grammatically acceptable sequence. But it will soon become clear that "use" for Wittgenstein is a quite restrictive concept: it is "use *in*" specific verbal situations and exchanges and sequences, and "use" to do or to achieve something, "use" that always has consequences. It is this practical and purposive "use in the language" that becomes more and more unquestionably, as his arguments develop, the measure of meaning.

But that observation still does not communicate the strength and even the severity of Wittgenstein's formulation. For if "use in the language" is *not*, as we might initially have supposed, "all sorts of things," then a great deal of verbal behavior—all such behavior, for example, that seems purposeless or inconsequential or, in Wittgenstein's terms, "idling"—cannot be considered "meaningful." The consequences of this exclusion, as we shall see, are enormous for how we think about language, and especially for how we conceive linguistic process in literary studies. And we shall also see, I think, that a similarly severe restriction of what "meaning" can be said to be is produced by the second important analogy for verbal activity given in the *Investigations*—and which also seems a "liberal" one—the famous connection between language and *games*.

Wittgenstein first draws this relation between language and "those games by means of which children learn their native language" and says that he will "sometimes speak of a primitive language as a language-game" (PI, 7). But as he continues, the concept flexes and enlarges to cover all sorts of verbal sequences and systems, and to become more and more important in identifying what he will consider as meaningful linguistic behavior. Thus, like the concept of meaning as *use*, the model of verbal activity as *game* seems initially most valuable for its variousness, even though it seems also to imply, at least, that language use is generally a matter of particular context and has meaning within a fixed familiar system in which rules of some sort are naturally involved. But even this last inference, it soon turns out, is weakened by the complication of just what a "game" might be.

> We can easily imagine people amusing themselves in a field by playing with a ball so as to start various existing games, but playing many without finishing them and in between throwing the ball aimlessly into the air, chasing one another with the ball and bombarding one another for a joke and so on. And now someone says: The whole time they are playing a ball-game and following definite rules at every throw.
>
> And is there not also the case where we play and—make up the rules as we go along? And there is even one where we alter them—as we go along?
>
> I said that the application of a word is not everywhere bounded by rules. But what does a game look like that is everywhere bounded by rules? whose rules never let a doubt creep in, but stop up all the cracks where it might?—Can't we imagine a rule determining the application of a rule, and a doubt which *it* removes—and so on?
>
> But that is not to say that we are in doubt because it is possible for us to *imagine* a doubt. . . .
>
> A rule stands there like a sign-post.—Does the sign-post leave no doubt open about the way I have to go? (PI, 83–85)

It thus appears that one of the more important inferences—if not the most important one—yielded by the connection of language with games is that there is a certain indeterminacy common to them both. They have their rules, but these rules do not rule out doubt, and neither do they presuppose any particular "application." At this point it may begin to seem that there is something rather too vague about the borders of the city of language, something too elastic about the dimensions of Wittgenstein's linguistic "tool-box." But he anticipates both that notion and the objections that accompany it. He admits that he has "nowhere said what the essence of a language-game, and hence of language, is," and he continues with a long list of "games" that is designed to show how many different sorts there are, how the concept of "game" is multiple and complex, and how it is used to describe all sorts of activities that resemble and differ from each other in all kinds of ways and seem connected only by what he calls "family resemblances" (PI, 67).

Our probable disappointment at the irregularities of the "game" model of language and its apparent insufficiency for explanatory purposes may be compensated by our recognition of how descriptively accurate a model it is, how good a conceptual match "game" and "language" are, especially in the ways in which both seem energized, and not enervated, by certain inexactnesses. For both games and language appear to thrive upon unboundedness.

> For how is the concept of a game bounded? What still counts as a game and what no longer does? Can you give the boundary? No. You can *draw* one; for none has so far been drawn. (But that never troubled you before when you used the word "game.")
>
> "But then the use of the word is unregulated, the 'game' we play with it is unregulated."—It is not everywhere circumscribed by rules; but no more are there any rules for how high one throws the ball in tennis, or how hard; yet tennis is a game for all that and has rules too. (PI, 68)

> How should we explain to someone what a game is? I imagine that we should describe *games* to him, and we might add: "This *and similar things* are called 'games.'" And do we know any more about it ourselves? Is it only other people whom we cannot tell exactly what a game is?—But this is not ignorance. We do not know the boundaries because none have been drawn. To repeat, we can draw a boundary—for a special purpose. Does it take that to make the concept usable? Not at all! . . . (PI, 69)

> One might say that the concept "game" is a concept with blurred edges.—"But is a blurred concept a concept at all?"—Is an indistinct photograph a picture of a person at all? Is it even always an advantage to replace an indistinct picture by a sharp one? Isn't the indistinct one often exactly what we need?
>
> Frege compares a concept to an area and says that an area with vague boundaries cannot be called an area at all. This presumably means that we cannot do anything with it.—But is it senseless to say: "Stand roughly there"? (PI, 71)

This seems to me a remarkable moment in the history of our thinking about language. The boundlessness, the blurredness, and the vagueness of the concept of "game" as an analogy for language are consequences of the *particular* natures of games. And they are so in two ways: first, there is such a wide variety of games that no conceptual "bounds" can contain them, and, second, the bounds or rules that apply to a particular game—which may be *conceptually* vague—become clear enough in its actual playing out. And it is because of this last consideration that Wittgenstein locates the meaning of verbal processes within their particular and active functioning.

In this way the flexibility of the "game" model for linguistic activity, even though unsatisfactory for explanatory purposes, seems fruitful, since it allows for the fine-tuning of rules to actual situations and acknowledges the immediacy and spontaneity of language-game sequences. But before we are quite taken with the particularity—and what I have called the "liberalness"—of Wittgenstein's view of our verbal behavior, we should attend more thoroughly to the negative implications of the language-game analogue, and the most important one of these is a corollary of the notion that the rules of language-games are enacted and embedded in their local playing out, that these rules have no *meaningful* existence anywhere else. The paradigms that give our language meaning do so only in the specific verbal conditions where they may occur; they receive their full articulation only within those conditions; and hence they cannot be said to exist apart from them.

> What do I call "the rule by which he proceeds"?—The hypothesis that satisfactorily describes his use of words, which we observe; or the rule which he looks up when he uses signs; or the one which he gives us in reply if we ask him what his rule is?—But what if observation does not enable us to see any clear rule, and the question brings none to light?—For he did indeed give me a definition when I asked him what he understood by "N," but he was prepared to withdraw and alter it.—So how am I to determine the rule according to which he is playing? He does not know it himself.—Or, to ask a better question: What meaning is the expression "the rule by which he proceeds" supposed to have left to it here? (PI, 82)

Apparently none—apart from the various ways it might have been actually involved in the particular playing of the language-game. Whatever form or whatever role the rule of a language-game may take, our access to it is only within the particular action of the particular game, and the capacity of the rule to give sense to a verbal sequence is revealed in and inseparable from the enactment of that capacity. In this way, rules are tied inextricably to their *applications*.[1]

Now this might seem, to some, a simple enough—and even a self-evident—observation. We may see how strong a claim it is, however, if we consider that if rules are inseparably entwined—so far as their fully articulated ruling force is concerned—with their particular applications, then they no longer may inhabit the spaces to which they have been traditionally assigned; they are neither in the mind of the game-player nor in some more general or essential order of existence, some Platonic supergrammar of forms and ideas. Of course, one may *think* generally about rules, just as one may abstract rules from games and fix them in "pure" form. But neither sort of imagining may be sufficiently indicative of their detailed working capacity in the cases in question: "What is essential to see is that the same thing can come before our minds when we hear the word and the application still be different. Has it the same meaning both times? I think we shall say not" (PI, 140). This as I see it is one of Wittgenstein's most important conceptions, this relocation of rules and paradigms—once more, in their articulated and functioning character—from the individual mind, or from the metaphysical order of such mental presences as "ideas," to the sites of their actual applications. And one of its correlates is the more obviously remarkable and consequential conception that our "mental" or imaginative *experience* as we use a word is irrelevant to whatever meaning is generated.

Thus, we may see, again, how what appeared to be a flexible and accommodating model of human linguistic behavior—this idea of the language-game—a model whose acknowledgment of particular variations from one case to another seemed both its strongest and weakest feature, is in fact a severe conception indeed. The notion that what we "mean" need have nothing to do with what goes on in our minds is antithetical to the fundamental assumptions of all sorts of linguistic disciplines and programs, of course, but to none of these more than to the principles of literary studies, where it has long been presumed that "meaning" is a function and even a property of the "mind" and more specifically of the imagination.

But to understand more clearly just what critique of literary studies Wittgenstein's thinking may amount to, it will be useful to examine his treatment of what is presumably an obviously literary matter: what it is that we do when we read. Of course, his fundamental interest in this activity is not literary or aesthetic, but is connected to the investigations I have been describing of how the rules of language-games function. More specifically, he is scrutinizing the proposition that "reading" is one sort of thing, either a "particular process" within the individual mind or some characteristic sort of behavior to be identified by a fixed and transcendental grammatical model. Therefore, he limits his inquiry, at first, to the simplest and most observable cases of "reading," where even "understanding" need not be in question: "First I need to remark that I am not counting the understanding of what is read as part of 'reading' for purposes of this investigation: reading here is the activity of rendering out loud what is written or printed; and also of writing from dictation, writing out something printed, playing from a score, and so on" (PI, 156). He is not considering the "understanding of what is read" here because he is initially interested in a different question: how we understand someone to be reading. But we shall see later that this question has significant ramifications for a reader's own "understanding," since "how we know someone to be reading" extends to "how we know someone to be understanding something." At this stage, however, Wittgenstein's genius for imagining particular cases and recognizing their limits both leads to and fills out an inference characteristic of his philosophy: that we "use the word 'to read' for a family of cases. And in different circumstances we apply different criteria for a person's 'reading'" (PI, 164). Yet he also, provisionally, continues to allow more "essential" questions: "But surely—we should like to say—reading is a quite particular process! Read a page of print and you can see that something special is going on, something highly characteristic.—Well, what does go on when I read the page?" (PI, 165)

Wittgenstein's usual answer to propositions in the form of "X is a particular process" is that "you are thinking of a particular process of X." It is such discriminative particularity in his inquiry into "what goes on" in reading that takes him through a series of comparative differences, and in this immediate instance to the difference between reading "arbitrary" marks and normal printed lines. And this difference yields further ones.

> Again, our eye passes over printed lines differently from the way it passes over arbitrary pothooks and flourishes. (I am not speaking here of what can be established by observing the movement of the eyes of a reader.) The eye passes, one would like to say, with particular ease, without being held up; and yet it doesn't *skid*. And at the same time involuntary speech goes on in the imagination. That is how it is when I read German and other languages, printed or written, and in various styles.—But what in all this is essential to reading as such? Not any one feature that occurs in all cases of reading. (PI, 168)

Then, once more, he allows another, more "theoretical" question: isn't there something common to all reading, some causal process that always occurs? He rejects the notion of "causation" at once, as something only to be established by the observation of regular concomitance, not something we might "feel," and he continues: "One might rather say, I feel that the letters are the *reason* why I read such-and-such. For if someone asks me, 'Why do you read such-and-such?'—I justify my reading by the letters which are there" (PI, 169). But such "justifications," he adds, are something that one *says*, after the fact, not what one *feels*, at the time, when one reads.

This last observation contains an important implication for literary studies: that what we say about reading is often merely an after-the-fact "justification" that only appears to describe the actual experience. And what we can say that is immediately relevant to that experience continues to diminish as Wittgenstein continues his interrogation: "I should like to say: when I read I feel a kind of *influence* of the letters working on me—but I feel no influence from that series of arbitrary flourishes" (PI, 169). How meager a yield this may appear: when I read I feel a kind of influence. And yet even it turns out to be excessive: "It would never have occurred to us to think that we *felt the influence* of letters on us when reading, if we had not compared the case of letters with that of arbitrary marks. And here we are indeed noticing a *difference*. And we interpret it as the difference between being influenced and not being influenced" (PI, 170). "Essential ingredients" of the reading experience continue to be observable only when one is examining that experience in one or another specifically—but often covertly—comparative way: "I might have used other words to hit off the experience I have when I read a word. Thus I might say that the written word *intimates* the sound to me.—Or again, that when one reads, letter and sound form a unity—as it were an alloy" (PI, 171). And if the resulting, various impressions seem not a substantial enough answer to the question of what "reading" really is, we soon discover that the end-result of this inquiry is even less satisfying.

> But now just read a few sentences in print as you usually do when you are not thinking about the concept of reading; and ask yourself whether you had such experiences of unity, of being influenced and the rest, as you read.—Don't say you had them unconsciously! Nor should we be misled by the picture which suggests that these phenomena came in sight "on closer inspection." If I am supposed to describe how an object looks from far off, I don't make the description more accurate by saying what can be noticed about the object on closer inspection. (PI, 171)

Once again, some fundamental assumptions and practices of literary studies and criticism may seem here to be under extreme interrogative pressure. It may be obvious, for instance, that this attitude toward "closer inspection" calls into question the generally accepted mode of literary analysis that we call "close reading," as if such "closeness" could always be suspected of falsifying not only the data but also the overall quality of the reading experience, which might actually occur, somehow, "far off." Whatever it was when it happened, this experience was not originally the thing produced by our means of measuring it.

Are we to infer from Wittgenstein's arguments here that the actual "experience" of reading itself is unapproachable, and that our efforts to describe this experience are about nothing that we could describe? Not exactly. He says, once again, only that such an experience is not one essential sort of thing, that all manner of activities might go on when one reads, but that these would not determine whether one was "reading" or not. Reading not only need not be any particular experience; it also need not be any experience at all, and still it could be reading. If, in other words, we bring this problem of reading as a mental experience into line with Wittgenstein's expressed attitudes about such experience elsewhere, we discover not that he doubts that it occurs but that he doubts its connection to the "meaning" of what one does. The meaning of reading—either the meaning that one gets while reading or the meaning of the observation that someone is reading—is not necessarily connected to any mental or imaginative experience the reader might have.

Wittgenstein's effort in this investigation of reading, then, as in his investigation of linguistic behavior more generally, is not to prove that there is nothing whatever going on in our minds when we read language—or speak or hear it—not to prove that there is no such thing as a "mental process" in relation to words. His claim is rather that what happens in our minds as we use language is never necessarily relevant to or restrictive upon its meaning. It is not our "thinking" along with words, as we say or hear them, that makes them work. Even more strikingly, as Wittgenstein extends this argument, it is not even any singularly preparatory thinking about them that can be said to give them the form they take.

> What happens when we make an effort—say in writing a letter—to find the right expression for our thoughts?—This phrase compares the process to one of translating or describing: the thoughts are already there (perhaps were there in advance) and we merely look for their expression. This picture is more or less appropriate in different cases.—But can't all sorts of things happen here?—I surrender to a mood and the expression *comes*. Or a picture occurs to me and I try to describe it. Or an English expression occurs to me and I try to hit on the corresponding German one. Or I make a gesture, and ask myself: What words correspond to this gesture? And so on.

> This case is similar to the one in which someone imagines that one could not think a sentence with the remarkable word order of German or Latin just as it stands. One first has to think it, and then one arranges the words in that queer order. (A French politician once wrote that it was a peculiarity of the French language that in it words occur in the order in which one thinks them.)
>
> But didn't I already intend the whole construction of the sentence (for example) at its beginning? So surely it already existed in my mind before I said it out loud!—If it was in my mind, still it would not normally be there in some different word order. But here we are constructing a misleading picture of "intending," that is, of the use of this word. An intention is embedded in its situation, in human customs and institutions. If the technique of the game of chess did not exist, I could not intend to play a game of chess. In so far as I do intend the construction of a sentence in advance, that is made possible by the fact that I can speak the language in question. (PI, 335–37)

One of the most important features of these passages is the criticism that they imply of a most favored prejudice: our presumption that language is secondary to "thought," that thought is somehow more real or more pure than the "expression of it." The other great antagonist of this notion, other than Wittgenstein, is Maurice Merleau-Ponty.

> If speech presupposed thought, if talking were primarily a matter of meeting the object through a cognitive intention or through a representation, we could not understand why thought tends toward expression as toward its completion, why the most familiar thing appears indeterminate as long as we have not recalled its name, why the thinking subject himself is in a kind of ignorance of his thoughts so long as he has not formulated them for himself, or even spoken or written them, as is shown by the example of so many writers who begin a book without knowing exactly what they are going to put into it. A thought limited to existing for itself, independently of the constraints of speech and communication, would no sooner

> appear than it would sink into the unconscious, which means that it would not exist even for itself. (P, 177)

> Thought is no "internal thing," and does not exist independently of the world and of words. What misleads us in this connection, and causes us to believe in a thought which exists for itself prior to expression, is thought already constituted and expressed, which we can silently recall to ourselves, and through which we acquire the illusion of an inner life. (P, 183)

Of course, this idea that language dominates and even generates thought is not the same as Wittgenstein's conception here, although I think he would have agreed—some of the time—with Merleau-Ponty's proposition that thought is language-generated and language-dependent.[2] Certainly the latter's "illusion of an inner life" bears a striking resemblance to the "illustrated turns of speech" that we may apprehend, as Wittgenstein says, upon "looking into ourselves" (PI, 295). But Wittgenstein's method of inquiry—here and most usually—is logical rather than phenomenological, and he is not so much interested in what the shape and nature of thought might be as in how various conceptions of "thought" follow from how we use that word and, more important, in what that same use implies about the relation of thought, not to language, but to the meaning of language. And perhaps the sharpest extension of his more general attitude that the mental processes and experiences of a language-user need never be relevant to the meaning that he communicates or understands is Wittgenstein's conception that meaningful *intentions* must be realized within expressed verbal situations and their public possibilities. Here again, his philosophy of language seems to collide with some of the assumptions and practices of literary studies, perhaps more crucially than ever. For if "mental" intentions—or any other inward process or experience—are not something both separate from and validative of the meaning of verbal expressions, if these cannot be said to restrict or to define such meaning, then why in relation to *literary* expression have we been so often concerned with the minds of both authors and readers?

We may return, in an effort to answer this question, to the famous observation that "an intention is embedded in its situation, in human customs and institutions," and what immediately follows it: "If the technique of the game of chess did not exist, I could not intend to play a game of chess." Now here is another remark, from the *Blue Book*, that also employs the vehicle of chess and that may help to define Wittgenstein's conception of the relation of mental activities of all sorts to meaning: "I want to play chess, and a man gives the white king a paper crown, leaving the use of the piece unaltered, but telling me that the crown has a meaning to him in the game, which he can't express by rules. I say: 'as long as it doesn't alter the use of the piece, it hasn't what I call a meaning' " (BB, 65). If we think of the "white king" as a word—and surely that is one of his implications here—and if we think of the "paper crown" as everything in our imaginations that might precede and accompany our use of that word, then it may be very hard to accept the pronouncement, "it hasn't what I call a meaning."

For we may want to say that what that "paper crown" has—what the "mental" accompaniments of our words have—is certainly a "meaning." The fact is that there is an entire range of occasions on which we use the word "meaning" in just this way, that we have been taught to use the word to indicate all the associations personal to ourselves that might be called up by public concepts. What about, for example, all those high school English compositions whose required titles were "What X Means to Me," where "X" is "America" or "Success" or any other similarly large, floating concept? Was what we were asked then to talk about as a meaning not a meaning?

Not in Wittgenstein's terms. Once again we must recognize the penetration of his criterion of "use" into our verbal behavior; what does not "alter the use" of a word in a language-game cannot be called a "meaning." Here, however, we should remember clearly just what "use" means for Wittgenstein and consider that it is fundamentally connected with the *work* that language may do. Any investigation of how language means must restrict itself to how it actually, purposively, and consequentially works, for "the confusions which occupy us arise when language is like an engine idling, not when it is doing work" (PI, 132). But all this emphasis upon language's work and purposes should make us aware of a difference, a difference more important, perhaps, than any of those differences among our verbal behavior that Wittgenstein has described before. For in singling out the white king and his paper crown, what his opponent has done is to *isolate* that piece from play. I shall say much more, especially in the following chapter, about the consequences of the "isolation" of *language*. But here, in relation to the playing of the game and the working of words, those consequences are figured in the negative. A concept like "America," isolated from any particular, "ordinary" working, would have *no* meaning.

But this may make us think, in the interests of literary studies, of the "isolation" of literary expressions. Of course, there are some varieties of literature that would seem dedicated to certain work and purposes, that would seem to have been written to achieve something. But there are many more, as I see it, that cannot be so characterized; working to some singular consequence is not at all what these sorts of verbal form are up to. And this must mean that certain kinds of literary expression are not meaningful if as Wittgenstein insists we restrict the concept of meaning to purposive use.

Now, as I may have indicated, I think there are very good reasons for so restricting this concept. I think—though of course there are some linguistic philosophers who do not share this view—that Wittgenstein's logical demonstrations unassailably justify the assimilation of meaning to use. I would also suggest—and this is more important for my purposes—that excluding the concept of "meaning" from the discussion of certain literary forms both alleviates certain current theoretical confusions about "literary" expression and illuminates one's description of its peculiar dynamics. In the chapters that follow I shall try to show how this may be so.

But the problem that I now want to address again is this: why and how has the confusion I have marked arisen? If "mental" or "imaginative" experiences generally, and "intentions" in the mind specifically, are not determinant of or restrictive upon meaning, then why are we so inclined—so illogically inclined, as Wittgenstein sees it—to connect the idea of meaning with them? Or why, if notions like "intention" and "meaning" have their most natural and justifiable homes in ordinary language-games, do we carry them over—often to our intellectual discomfort—into our consideration of literary expression, where intentions seem imaginable mainly as obscure, psychological phenomena, and meaning as a hidden presence or power in the mind? And, finally, what features of literary expression seem both to invite and to elude this concern with "meanings" and "intentions," and how might these features be more fruitfully described?

The answers to these questions begin to grow with Wittgenstein's sustained attention, both in *Philosophical Investigations* and in *Remarks on the Philosophy of Psychology*, to linguistic phenomena that might, at least initially, seem more "mental." And they seem so because—unlike more purposive verbal activities—they involve complex imaginings that are describable as "experiences" in a way that the processes of working language are not. This sort of case is first exposed in the remarkable sequence in the *Investigations* that concerns "seeing an aspect."

It is important to note at the beginning of this set of considerations that seeing, or noticing, an "aspect" of something for Wittgenstein involves a perceptual doubleness, for it has elements both of constancy and change: "I contemplate a face, and then suddenly notice its likeness to another. I *see* that it has not changed; and yet I see it differently. I call this experience 'noticing an aspect'" (PI, p. 193). What is therefore in question here is not habitual or accustomed perception. If one sees the "duck-rabbit"—a sketch that resembles both the profiled representations of a duck's head and a rabbit's head—always only as a duck or a rabbit, then he is not "seeing an aspect" of it.

> It would have made as little sense for me to say "Now I am seeing it as . . ." as to say at the sight of a knife and fork "Now I am seeing this as a knife and fork." This expression would not be understood.—Any more than: "Now it's a fork" or "It can be a fork too."
>
> One doesn't "*take*" what one knows as the cutlery at a meal *for* cutlery; any more than one ordinarily tries to move one's mouth as one eats, or aims at moving it. (PI, p. 195)

It is no accident, of course, that "aspect seeing" is most easily ruled out in the case of utensils, whose "use" is obviously the most important and usually the only consideration. Given Wittgenstein's connection of "use" with meaning, therefore, we may begin to suspect that this "seeing of aspects" will not be a matter of "meaning."

But his treatment of more ordinary apprehensions as a contrast to the seeing of aspects may also clarify for us something that is too often mistaken: just what "ordinary" means in phrases like "ordinary language." For here our "ordinary" purposes with utensils have two obvious characteristics: first, those purposes seem to be "habitual," to involve verbal and perceptual processes that have been learned and fixed, and that by virtue of the invariance of the language-games in which they customarily occur yield no options. But the second characteristic of these "ordinary" processes is more important than the first, for it indicates, among other things, that "habitual" here need not mean "thoughtless" in the sense of "automatic" or unconscious; it is not that there must be no language—or whatever else—in our heads when we are engaged in ordinary behaviors, verbal or otherwise, but rather that in these behaviors, just as utensils are subservient to the uses made of them, language is dominated by *action*. In these "ordinary" situations, language seems always to take a backseat, to efface its own "presence" in favor of getting something done. Words seem important *only* in these ordinary cases for their contribution to their purposive sequence. And thus, from another angle, we may see why their "existence" in one's mind or anywhere else is irrelevant in ordinarily meaningful cases.

But the sort of perception and behavior—and, as we shall see, of linguistic activity—discovered in Wittgenstein's treatment of "changes of aspect" is another thing entirely. Here multiplicity of perception does seem to suggest the importance of something "in the mind." If the perceived object does not change, and yet one sees something different in it, then surely something else has changed, and the "mind" is the most favored candidate.

> But what is different: my impression? my point of view?—Can I say? I *describe* the alteration like a perception; quite as if the object has altered before my eyes.
>
> "Now I am seeing *this*," I might say (pointing to another picture, for example). This has the form of a report of a new perception.

> The expression of a change of aspect is the expression of a *new* perception and at the same time of the perception's being unchanged. (PI, pp. 195–96)

This doubleness or complexity is not to be explained, however, by imagining something like the object located *only* "in the mind": "And above all do *not* say 'After all my visual impression isn't the *drawing*; it is *this*—which I can't shew to anyone.'—Of course it is not the drawing, but neither is it anything of the same category, which I carry within myself" (PI, p. 196). Yet if we do not imagine some such contrast between inner and outer, between "mental objects" and real ones, that might generate the multiplicity we feel in noticing a change of aspect, then how do we explain this phenomenon? How do we account for a kind of "perception" that fluctuates but remains constant, that yields differences while somehow remaining the same? What is it that remains the same here—the object "itself"? But that might seem to change with every look. How then, or where, is it the "same"?

It is this sort of perceptual experience, I think, beyond all others that may lead us to imagine essential and singular models or structures, located usually in the mind—and of which "intentions" are only one variety—that establish or constitute what is constant within our shifting and even contradictory perceptions of the "same" things. The difficulty of accounting for complex perceptions without recourse to such mentalistic metaphysics becomes evident in the ensuing stages of Wittgenstein's inquiry, and what puzzles him most is that this act of "seeing an aspect" seems like seeing and yet cannot be classified strictly as perception; "the flashing of an aspect on us seems half visual experience, half thought."

> I meet someone whom I have not seen for years; I see him clearly, but fail to know him. Suddenly I know him, I see the old face in the altered one. I believe that I should do a different portrait of him now if I could paint.
>
> Now, when I know my acquaintance in a crowd, perhaps after looking in his direction for quite a while,—is this a special sort of

> seeing? Is it a case of both seeing and thinking? or an amalgam of the two, as I should almost like to say?
>
> The question is: *why* does one want to say this? (PI, p. 197)

The argumentative developments that follow this question are remarkable, both for the conclusions reached and for their display of Wittgenstein's investigative capability. He considers the "aspects of a triangle" and how it

> can be seen as a triangular hole, as a solid, as a geometrical drawing; as standing on its base, as hanging from its apex; as a mountain, as a wedge, as an arrow or pointer, as an overturned object which is meant to stand on the shorter side of the right angle, as a half parallelogram, and as various other things.
>
> "You can think now of *this* now of *this* as you look at it, can regard it now as *this* now as *this*, and then you will see it now *this* way, now *this*."—*What* way? There is no further qualification.
>
> But how is it possible to *see* an object according to an *interpretation*?—The question represents it as a queer fact; as if something were being forced into a form it did not really fit. But no squeezing, no forcing took place here. (PI, p. 200)

So the previous "amalgam" of seeing and thinking has become seeing "according to an interpretation." Next he leads us—though it would be as correct to say that he leads himself, since his progress is so genuinely inquiring—to the notion that "interpretative" seeing may relate to imaginative "potential": "How would the following account do: 'What I can see something *as*, is what it can be a picture of'?" (PI, p. 201)

The crucial moment in the sequence, however, occurs when he is considering again the aspects of the triangle in order to show that a certain fundamental knowledge must be in our possession before we can see aspects:

> In the triangle I can see now *this* as apex, *that* as base—now *this* as apex, *that* as base.—Clearly the words "Now I am seeing *this* as the apex" cannot so far mean anything to a learner who has only just

> met the concepts of apex, base, and so on.—But I do not mean this as an empirical proposition.
>
> "Now he's seeing it like *this*," "now like *that*" would only be said of someone *capable* of making certain applications of the figure quite freely.
>
> The substratum of this experience is the mastery of a technique.
>
> But how queer for this to be the logical condition of someone's having such-and-such an *experience*! After all, you don't say that one only "has toothache" if one is capable of doing such-and-such.—From this it follows that we cannot be dealing with the same concept of experience here. It is a different though related concept.
>
> It is only if someone *can do*, has learnt, is master of, such-and-such, that it makes sense to say he has had *this* experience.
>
> And if this sounds crazy, you need to reflect that the *concept* of seeing is modified here. (A similar consideration is often necessary to get rid of a feeling of dizziness in mathematics.)
>
> We talk, we utter words, and only *later* get a picture of their life. (PI, pp. 208–9)

Thus, Wittgenstein has achieved a perspective that seems to ease the previously troubling paradox that seeing an aspect seems an "experience" but at the same time depends upon "thinking" or "interpretation," for it now appears that this "thinking" is past, a "knowledge" or "competence" that has already been established and which can come collectedly into play in perception. The resulting experience is different from that of a toothache—"a different though related concept"—but it is an experience nonetheless.

But then he takes a further step—or leap—that is startling in its connection of seeing aspects with *verbal* behavior, and I quote it again: "We talk, we utter words, and only *later* get a picture of their life." His examination of the perception of aspects, of the capacity of that perception to generate variation from a single and constant object, has now been shifted to expose two sorts of *linguistic* activity. This connection seems so potentially interesting that we may not notice that it reveals one of Wittgenstein's presumptions about the "seeing of aspects" more generally: for if this sort of perception can be related to a sort of verbal behavior, then it would seem to depend—in the same way that language does—much more upon the "external" features of the perceived object than upon some mental process or condition. This is not to say that "mental" concepts are irrelevant here—as they may be in ordinary perception and speech—but that the active perceptual complexity of seeing aspects, and now a similar complexity in relation to *words*, is much more "objectively" built-in, a matter of how the aspected image or word is *presented* to be *recognized* rather than of how complicatedly we might "think" about something that is in itself simple.

I shall return to this conception, for it bears sharply upon what I shall call the "grammatical" presentation of language whose "aspects" we see. For the moment, however, it is necessary to clarify the two sorts of verbal behavior that Wittgenstein is considering at this stage in his arguments. Our *competence* to "talk" is one sort: our capability to use and understand language in ways that are "ordinary," that is, purposive and efficient and *experienceless*. But the other sort, the verbal equivalent of seeing aspects, is quite different, for here one's response to a word—given his prior competence in the use of the word—may occur as a kind of experience.

> I can imagine some arbitrary cipher . . . to be a strictly correct letter of some foreign alphabet. Or again, to be a faultily written one, and faulty in this way or that: for example, it might be slapdash, or typical childish awkwardness, or like the flourishes in a legal document. It could deviate from the correctly written letter in a variety of ways.—And I can see it in various aspects according to the fiction I surround it with. And here there is a close kinship with "experiencing the meaning of a word." (PI, p. 210)

"Experiencing the meaning of a word," then, involves the awareness of surrounding "fictions," which, given that this awareness depends upon linguistic *competence*, I take to be a multiple recognition of that word's meanings in various language-games, meanings that, because they are multiple aspects of an isolated word or set of words, do not function as meaning ordinarily does. Very early in the *Investigations*, when Wittgenstein suggested that our utterances are often intelligible by virtue of their contrast with other possible utterances, it was not to suggest that we actively imagine those other possibilities: "But what does using one sentence in contrast with others consist in? Do the others, perhaps, hover before one's mind? . . . No" (*PI*, 20). His consistent skepticism regarding such imaginative "presences" in connection with ordinarily meaningful language renders such a question unmistakably rhetorical. But in the extraordinarily verbal condition that we are now considering, contrasting possibilities may indeed "hover before one's mind" as one utters or responds to a word.

> Suppose someone said: every familiar word, in a book for example, actually carries an atmosphere with it in our minds, a "corona" of lightly indicated uses.—Just as if each figure in a painting were surrounded by delicate shadowy drawings of scenes, as it were in another dimension, and in them we saw the figures in different contexts.—Only let us take this assumption seriously!—Then we see that it is not adequate to explain *intention*.
>
> For if it is like this, if the possible uses of a word do float before us in half-shades as we say or hear it—this simply goes for *us*. But we communicate with other people without knowing if they have this experience too.[3]

In this beautiful and brilliant passage—those figures in the painting "surrounded by delicate shadowy drawings" may remind one, in both phrase and concept, of Nabokov at his best—Wittgenstein's first priority, as always, is to describe the conditions and process of language's meaning, and here specifically to show that no such "experience" of a word's "atmosphere" is "adequate to explain *intention*." And he has demonstrated thoroughly, as we have seen, not only that we may "communicate with other people without knowing if they have this experience," this same sense of a word's "corona" of possible meanings as we do, but also that we may communicate without having any such experience ourselves. He has shown that this experience both is not necessary to meaning and does not necessarily ever take place in us when meaningful communication occurs. This conception is summed very neatly just a few lines on from the preceding quotation: "The meaning of a word is not the experience one has in hearing or saying it, and the sense of a sentence is not a complex of such experiences." But it is also clear by now that these *experiences* of language are extremely important to Wittgenstein, that this perception of a word's "atmosphere" of "lightly indicated uses" is quite real, and because it is so real, it is perhaps the one feature of our relation to language that most confuses us when we try to think about how words mean, about "communication."

I shall try in subsequent chapters to demonstrate how in certain literary situations we may "take this assumption" that words have an "atmosphere" quite seriously indeed, how by various grammatical arrangements they may seem both to be removed or isolated from use and to be surrounded by their "possible uses." In the passage at hand, Wittgenstein's proposal that the "atmosphere" of a word *might* be conceived as he suggests is hypothetical and general; it is not connected to any particular example of verbal construction that would make such a recognition inescapable. But what is most important to understand here is the conception that if, on any particular occasion, this *were* so for us, and words were felt to be surrounded by "different contexts," then there would occur a living connection between two sets of linguistic phenomena that for philosophical purposes must be kept strictly separate. For the "uses" of words would thus seem evidently involved in *both* "meaning" and "experiencing meaning," though involved very differently; and that difference would be between actual, functioning uses of words and their "possible uses."[4]

This connection between two quite different verbal processes—between language's meaning and the experience of its possible meanings—amounts very often for us, as I have suggested, to trouble. Indeed, it may be seen as the source of our greatest linguistic confusions, ranging from our constantly mistaking the experienced *effects* of words for their meanings in day-to-day life—at one end of the scale—to our now traditional efforts to explain the intense and complex experience of certain literary forms in terms of meaning—at the other end. And as Wittgenstein proceeds with his investigation of this "experience of meaning," or "experience of language," we may see that our confusion is justifiable, or at any rate that it is matched to some degree by the difficulty he himself has in keeping separate these two sorts of verbal process or conditions that he has demonstrated to be so radically different.

Their difference is still obvious in his next step, which is to show that the two linguistic behaviors in question are not equally possible in the language of any situation, nor are they equally possible to all human beings. For even if a certain competence with words is the precondition for experiencing their "life," this competence does not entail such experience, for we can imagine people who might be capable of the first but not the second: "The question now arises: Could there be human beings lacking in the capacity to see something *as something*—and what would that be like?"

> Aspect-blindness will be *akin* to the lack of a "musical ear."

> The importance of this concept lies in the connexion between the concepts of "seeing an aspect" and "experiencing the meaning of a word." For we want to ask "What would you be missing if you did not *experience* the meaning of a word?"
>
> What would you be missing, for instance, if you did not understand the request to pronounce the word "till" and to mean it as a verb,—or if you did not feel that a word lost its meaning and became a mere sound if it was repeated ten times over? (PI, pp. 213–14)

Of course, he has already suggested a direction for the effort to answer such questions.

> Here it occurs to me that in conversation on aesthetic matters we use the words: "You have to see it like *this*, this is how it is meant"; "When you see it like *this*, you see where it goes wrong"; "You have to hear this bar as an introduction"; "You must hear it in this key"; "You must phrase it like *this*" (which can refer to hearing as well as to playing). (PI, p. 202)

> If you feel the seriousness of a tune, what are you perceiving? (PI, p. 210)

The trend of these examples is characteristic. As Wittgenstein continues, it most frequently appears that what we would be missing if we could not see the aspects of words, *experience* their meaning, is most easily exposed by aesthetic examples, something that we most obviously get from poetry, or from music. And though I shall often maintain in what follows that this experience is by no means limited to "aesthetic" cases, I shall also show—especially in the chapter on "voice"—that Wittgenstein's concentration upon "musical" perceptions here, and more specifically upon the sounded forms of words as accesses to the experience of their meanings, is fundamentally significant, that the sounds of language—especially when isolated from use by aesthetic conditions—are often crucial to a most vital perception of grammatical possibility.

But these "aesthetic" examples, and especially the literary ones, begin to cause trouble: " 'When I read a poem or narrative with feeling, surely something goes on in me which does not go on when I merely skim the lines for information' " (PI, p. 214). "Surely," and we have observed his rigorous demonstration that that "something" is both undoubtable and describable. But then he must immediately ask here, "What processes am I alluding to?" and list the various actions he might take with the words so as to get the reading of them right: such as hearing the "ring" of the sentences, or paying "careful attention" to "intonation," or imagining a "picture" that helps him to read with the "correct expression."

Now the difficulty here, I think—and it is a hazardous one—is that many, though certainly not all, of these "processes" might serve in a case where one wanted to communicate an ordinary, but subtle or fine, *meaning*, even though Wittgenstein is presumably citing them to describe an *experience* of reading where achieved meaning is not at all in question.[5] The consequent ambiguity is similar to that which we find in a remark that seems primarily directed the other way, not at literary expression or the experience of words, but at language's meaningful or communicative functioning, despite the fact that the analogy is with music: "Understanding a sentence is much more akin to understanding a theme in music than one may think" (PI, 527). Here the concern *seems* to be with getting the sentence "just right," with the effects of "rhythm" and "pattern" upon the precise comprehension of a perhaps difficult concept. But of course this same quotation might also be used to support the quite different case for the experience of language; for the fact is that

Wittgenstein employs the word "understanding" in two contrary ways, especially in the later stages of the *Investigations*. One of these, of course, implies knowing what someone or something means in ordinary communication; the other implies a grasp of—or at least a participation in—a certain sort of experience, or a sensitivity to the feeling or atmosphere or possibilities of words: "Then has 'understanding' two different meanings here?—I would rather say that these kinds of use of 'understanding' make up its meaning, make up my *concept* of understanding. For I *want* to apply the word 'understanding' to all this" (PI, 532).

I shall return to this dichotomous and problematic sense of "understanding" more than once. But at the moment my interest is in why Wittgenstein seems at times so clear and assured at such a concept's double duty, while at others he seems strained and even confused about it: "When I pronounce this word while reading with expression it is completely filled with its meaning.—'How can this be, if meaning is in the use of the word?' Well, what I said was intended figuratively. Not that I chose the figure: it forced itself on me.—But the figurative employment of the word can't get into conflict with the original one" (PI, p. 215). Is the word that is "figuratively employed" here "*meaning*"? And why is that usage "figurative," when the experiential and noncommunicative sense of "understanding" was not, but a legitimate and literal part of the concept? And—whether "figurative" or not—surely *this* employment of "meaning" does "get into conflict" with the other one. It is this very conflict, it seems fair to say, that most occupies Wittgenstein in his philosophy.[6]

Of course, one might read that "can't" as a logical "mustn't"—though that seems a doubtful reading—and thus take this paragraph to say that "to mean" and "to be full of meaning" must be kept conceptually separate, a proposition that is evidently correct and useful. But "can't" has contradictory implications here of both a complacency and an urgency that seem inappropriate to such a logical point. More and more frequently in these later stages of the *Investigations* it seems as if two sides of Wittgenstein's mind were in dialogue with each other, one insisting that meaning is defined only in actual and purposive usage, that it is different from the "feeling" or the "point" or the "effect" of words in that it need never depend upon anyone's having any sort of simultaneous, corresponding "experience," and the other insisting upon the force and weight of this experience of language and its life, and demonstrating a finely tuned and even painful sensitivity to the aspects of words that compose it.

> If a sensitive ear shews me, when I am playing this game, that I have now *this* now *that* experience of the word—doesn't it also shew me that I often do not have *any* experience of it in the course of talking?—For the fact that I then also mean it, intend it, now like *this* now like *that*, and maybe also say so later is, of course, not in question.
>
> But the question now remains why, in connexion with this *game* of experiencing a word, we also speak of "the meaning" and of "meaning it."—This is a different kind of question.—It is the phenomenon which is characteristic of this language-game that in *this* situation we use this expression: we say we pronounced the word with *this* meaning and take this expression over from that other language-game.
>
> Call it a dream. It does not change anything. (*PI*, pp. 215–16)

The second paragraph of this passage, especially near its end, may seem to obscure as much as it clarifies. In the first paragraph, "meaning" and "intending" the word, even though that usage might vary through a sequence of expressions—"now like this now like that"—is considered obviously "ordinary," and thus distinguishable from having a *various experience* of a word, so that the former is "not in question" when we are discussing the latter. When we say, however, that "meaning" or "intention" seems to "fill" a word—when "now like *this* now like *that*" implies not a sequence but a simultaneity, a complex and integral variation somehow isolated in the word itself—then we are considering quite a different sort of case, a case in which more than one "use" seems immediately present in the word or phrase we apprehend. "Fullness of meaning" is undeniably a *singular* perception, however, and thus we may imagine, by misanalogy with ordinary cases, that its "meanings" or "intentions" should be singular—or reducible to the singular—as well. But this wholeness or concentratedness of the experience of meaning is not the same as singleness of meaning or intention. Indeed, neither meaning nor intention in its ordinary functioning is in question here, no more than is "use." So much we have noted. But it does not finally seem clear in the passage in view whether Wittgenstein is talking about "meaning" or "fullness of meaning," though it appears to be the latter. He is concerned, to be sure, that the use of the concept of "meaning" here must be seen as unusual, concerned to insist that its home is in ordinary language. But this concern seems to have commited him to an example—"we pronounced the word with *this* meaning"—that does not fit where it is—connected to the experiencing of the aspects of words—for it reduces these aspects to one, and thus seems to refer to some exacting but nonetheless ordinary communication.

To call both the meaningful and the experiential processes of words "language-games," furthermore, is misleading, and dangerously so.[7] The analogy between language and games was initially founded, as we have seen, upon the way rules functioned for regulating, for rendering intelligible, particular verbal sequences. The thrust of "language-game" was local and specific and emphasized the immediate purposes and consequences of a sequence of behavior. Like a move in a game, the use of a word was designed to do something, employed toward a specific achievement.

But if the experiencing of language—and here I am thinking especially of that experience in literary forms of expression—is also to be called a "language-game," then that phrase must be read in an entirely different way, for this set of processes and conditions has none of the characteristics of ordinary language-games that I have just described. One might say, indeed, that the confusions of literary studies are most often produced by pressing for the attributes of ordinary language-games where they cannot be found. If, for example, we were to look in many sorts of texts for a meaning or intention "embedded in its situation," we could not find it, for these texts do not connect with any one such practical and purposive situation. (And thus we might turn to the "situation" of the author's mind.) Nor, in these same kinds of texts, is there the subordination of language to action that is characteristic of ordinary usage, but rather a reverse condition, where verbal substance and possibility takes all one's attention. In short, the varieties of literary expression that I have in mind—some of which I shall describe in the chapters to follow—are meaningless in comparison to ordinary language-games; the experience of them involves possible meanings and even intentions as it does "possible situations," and none of these is at all similar to its ordinary opposite number. It follows that this experience of language, and those linguistic forms that produce this experience, might better be considered as "possible language-games," or better yet, and to acknowledge the way in which a single such form—an entire text, for example—may imply a plurality of meaningful vocabularies, as a *display* of language-games, and throughout these discussions I shall try to demonstrate the usefulness of this concept.

But I do not want to insist any further on the difficulty of these ideas, nor on the strain that even Wittgenstein sometimes reveals in his efforts to describe wholly our mixed language and at the same time to distinguish among its divided and contrary processes and motives. He is clear about these matters almost all of the time, and at some moments when I think no one else could be, when no one else would pay the price that descriptive accuracy demands. That price, in one part, is a surrendering of theoretical ambition, a relinquishing of comprehensive explanation in favor of what actually can be descriptively known; but, in another, it is also the sacrificing, anywhere necessary, of his own remarkable sensitivity toward what he establishes as the experience of words, his feeling for the life of language, to a rigorous account of how that language means regardless of that experience.

That this was such a sacrifice is evident often in *Philosophical Investigations*, but nowhere more so than in the last line of the last quotation I gave: "Call it a dream. It does not change anything." For the inference that I draw here is that the "dream" in question is that of the experience of verbal possibility, and that Wittgenstein calls it a "dream," certainly, to show that it is not a matter of meaning, to mark its difference from practical and purposive usage, and to indicate that it is situationless and inconsequential. But dreams, as we know, have heavy effects upon our lives, even if these are not the "consequences" of meaning; and calling the experience of language a "dream," especially when that "does not change anything," seems to acknowledge such effects, and to acknowledge the substance and fascination of all those properties of language's process that may often seem more important than meaning and are so dangerous for philosophy, especially for a philosopher so concentrated upon what can be said about meaning itself.

In literary studies we have been neither so scrupulous nor so generous. For our inescapable perception that the apprehension of at least certain sorts of literary expressions is felt as "experience" has moved us not to efforts at describing them in those terms, but instead—perhaps in an attempt to justify our interest in such matters, or to bring that interest into line with the more practical motives of language at work or in business—to forced conflations of verbal experience with verbal meaning. Now one can imagine this as a strategy for, say, getting people to take poetry seriously; and one can also imagine the trivializing attitudes toward literature and literary criticism it may have been called up to combat. No doubt, as well, this confusion of "meaning" with "reading experience" has had some good and useful effects in the classroom, though I think that most of these could be had with more logical and consistent attention to what "meaning" really amounts to, and thus to how different from that the experience of reading may be.

But this mistake is understandable in another way as well: for how can we describe the experience even of a single word without distinguishing and fixing, one after another, its aspects, without transforming various possible uses perceived integrally in that word into a sequence of singular "interpretations," as if those were the sort of thing with which we began. This is a liability even for Empson, and despite the subtlety and precision of his reading, a liability of which he is well aware.

> Now I was frequently puzzled in considering my examples, though not quite in this way. I felt sure that the example was beautiful and that I had, broadly speaking, reacted to it correctly. But I did not at all know what had happened in this "reaction"; I did not know why the example was beautiful. And it seemed to me that I was able

> in some cases partly to explain my feelings to myself by teasing out the meanings of the text. Yet these meanings when teased out (in a major example) were too complicated to be remembered together as if in one glance of the eye; they had to be followed each in turn, as possible alternative reactions to the passage; and indeed there is no doubt that some readers sometimes do only get part of the full intention. In this way such a passage has to be treated as if it were ambiguous, even though it may be said that for a good reader it is only ambiguous (in the ordinary sense of the term) while he is going through an unnecessary critical exercise. (*STA*, x)

In calling into question the mode of description that has failed to measure the beauty of his examples and to comprehend his reading experience, Empson has given us a beautifully accurate expression of the insufficiency of accounting for a complex and unified experience of words as if it were a set of meanings, and of how describing grammatical possibilities one after another mistakes the experience of perceiving them. For the sequence of "alternative" meanings that results from such an effort must inevitably then be conceived as "ambiguous," whereas, in the condition in which one originally perceived them, these possibilities were not "ambiguous" at all but, as it were, complementary in composing the various experience of a word or phrase, whose wholeness and singularity was what was most evident. "Ambiguity" is a condition of meaning, an unstable and even a tense condition that seems to demand resolution. But in a display of grammatical possibilities no such reduction seems called for, since the language of that display itself already seems as concentrated as it could be. And thus one's method of description of one sort of verbal condition will have converted it to quite another one, and entirely transformed its actual quality, so much so that a sensibility even of Empson's powers must regret its responsive efforts as "an unnecessary critical exercise."

This mistaking of certain literary processes that Empson defines, and that he himself could identify but not avoid, is, as I have suggested, a misapprehension to which literary description is always liable. But it is impossible to prevent and even to detect if we approach literary expressions with meaning on our minds. The consequences, then, will be not only the theoretical confusions that I have alluded to, but also, and much more important, an insufficient recognition of what seems to me a great mystery: why it is that we respond so energetically to language that is evidently not meaningful, why it is that the exposure of human language and its possibilities to human beings is so much more enthralling for them than what language means.

CHAPTER TWO

Language As Such

> *Much* can be said about a fine aesthetic difference—this is very important. That is to say, the first utterance is of course merely "*This* word fits, *this* one does not" or the like; but then there may be discussion of all the widely ramified connexions made by each of these words. That is to say, it is not all over once that the first judgment has been made; rather what it depends on is the *field* of each word. (*RPP* 1:357)

What are the situations in which what I have called the "experience of language" occurs? What verbal arrangements—what sorts of grammatical structure—establish this more purely "grammatical" condition in which language is exposed or displayed, and how do these differ from verbal formations from which singular meanings seem to demand to be derived? And what, finally, are the characteristics of a reader's responsive action to these different sets of linguistic conditions? I want to begin this inquiry with a case in which that "action"—what a reader does with a text—may seem very active indeed, but not at all, as we shall see, in the way of realizing an experience of *language*.

> The taxi went up the hill, passed the lighted square, then on into the dark, still climbing, then levelled out onto a dark street behind St. Etienne du Mont, went smoothly down the asphalt, passed the trees and the standing bus at the Place de la Contrescarpe, then turned onto the cobbles of the Rue Mouffetard. (*SAR*, 25)

> It was a fine morning. The horse-chestnut trees in the Luxembourg gardens were in bloom. There was the pleasant early-morning feeling of a hot day. I read the papers with the coffee and then smoked a cigarette. The flower-women were coming up from the market and arranging their daily stock. Students went by going up to the law school, or down to the Sorbonne. The Boulevard was busy with trams and people going to work. (*SAR*, 35)

The first of these passages is an example of what we might think of as very detailed travel writing. But if we see that it fits that category not merely because it describes movements within the fictional space of the story but because it "travels" itself, because its construction urges a reader to "follow" it, then we might say that the second passage travels as well, even though its narrator is sitting still. Both passages seem "linear": the imagination proceeds along them. But why does it do so? Why does such writing seem to be composed of elements that function as steps, or as occasions for steps that a reader must take?

In the first passage names of the streets over which one moves may seem strange in themselves, even as if to require translation, and progress over or through them is at least in part an effort to get past unfamiliar words to known ones. But I would argue that we tend to treat the second passage, whose elements may be more familiar to us, in much the same way, and therefore that our motives in the first one have relatively little to do with our knowledge of Paris or of French. What is important is not so much how the terms of this passage differ from what we already know as how these terms differ from each other. It is that difference in both passages, that variation from one term to another—from St. Etienne du Mont to the Place de la Contrescarpe to the Rue Mouffetard; from morning to horse chestnut trees to gardens to bloom to hot day to papers to coffee to cigarette to flower women to students, and on—that drives one's imagination along. Linear grammar, then, the grammar that urges one to get *through* what he reads, is a grammar that insists upon verbal differentiation.

Hemingway's is one of the most efficient techniques we have for accomplishing this effect, precisely because it seems not "formed"; it is what one might call a "weak" grammar, whose phrasing often appears completely given over to presentation—by virtue of the verb "to be"—and to *temporal* sequence—there was this and then this and then this—and so allows for a maximum differentiation of its increments. In such a grammar there is very little in the way of subordination or logical structuring, for example, to interfere with a reader's free movement over such "free" sentences or to hinder the continuation of the variety that stimulates such movement.

But further to describe one's reading motives here would be more speculative. Is it that in stepping on and past these differing words we consider them familiarized, or assimilated, as if by analogy, even, with biological processes? Or is it that as they differ among themselves, they constitute almost "nervous" irritants to be smoothed or, more drastically, to be erased? To explain our verbal behavior by analogies to behaviors of other sorts is seldom interesting and never satisfying, if only because it seems such a reduction of evident linguistic life. All that we can say at this point is that verbal differentiation apparently generates the motive to get through, or to get over, as if to overcome, or to silence, its strangeness.

But surely there is more even to what seems a case of relatively simple reading than this: what about "meaning," and the understanding of it? It is precisely the question of what meaning is, and of what "understanding" amounts to in such cases, that we are asking: "We speak of understanding a sentence in the sense in which it can be replaced by another which says the same; but also in the sense in which it cannot be replaced by any other. (Any more than one musical theme can be replaced by another)" (PI, 531). The first sense of "understanding a sentence" that Wittgenstein remarks, in which that sentence "can be replaced by another," seems relevant to a large part of our activities with words. It is something that we may do, in the most obvious way, to get the meaning of foreign languages. In simple and literal cases of "translation," the understanding of the strange text is achieved by substituting for it, by replacing it with another language. And it may go without saying that this must involve an initial action of looking past or through the foreign text.

But the passages from Hemingway that I have quoted so far seemed to generate only that initial response. Unlike the case of simple translation, there is in this one no *presumed* more familiar language that we are driving toward as our imaginations move over and through this language. And the motive for this movement is not that the text as a whole is "foreign" but that it is strange within itself, in the way that its parts or elements continue to differ with each other. Still, it may be obvious that the effort to get from one part of these sentences to another, and then from one sentence to another, is a "translative" one, for it would seem to involve a determination upon *some* other, future language—a language that will assuage or erase the strangeness that grammatical differing presents. In the most obvious and literal cases of "translation," once again, this alternative language is presupposed, something that is available both before and after the questionable text. But in the case we are now considering, it seems something we are seeking, something hypothetical. This is to say that the motive for "following" a text always involves the feeling that the grass further on will be greener, that the shakiness of what presently bears our attention will become more familiar and solid. And this is what happens as each subsequent verbal increment replaces the one preceding it, but it only happens in retrospect. So long as the grammar of a text is varying and differential—so long as our reading is "linear"—the familiar language that we seek, and in whose interest we continue to replace one term with another, is only the language we have left behind, language of which we no longer have immediate apprehension. To put this another way, in such determinedly progressive reading, the language that we have passed acquires the solidity of something that has already happened, and even of something discarded. This is not the sort of language we were trying for, not the future and ultimate vocabulary that would clarify and satisfy; but it is all we can get. It is in this way that the last sentences of certain narratives may be the most intriguing and least satisfactory of all.

I do not suppose that the preceding argument is in any way exhaustive. Certainly the examples I have cited are not. There are many sorts of texts—many sorts of grammatical "differentiation"—where reading may primarily take this form of replacing one expression with a next and another in an effort ultimately to replace the whole thing with some other language entirely. But what I am trying to do is both to suggest a range for such texts and to scrutinize the near end of that range. The unfamiliarity of a German text, for example, and what we do about that, may be obvious. But to consider that we respond with similar motives to a sentence from Hemingway, which, by comparison, would seem utterly commonplace and comfortable, indicates something remarkable about how we come to our reading. It suggests, for one thing, that verbal expressions, no matter how well known their incremental parts, are always in their composition strange until proved otherwise, guilty until proved innocent. But it also suggests, of course, that we are confident such proof can be accomplished, that familiarity can be achieved.

If we return to Hemingway for a moment, we may see why this is so. For his grammar is, as I have suggested, a "weak grammar." There are many verbal forms for which this phrase might be appropriate, of course, that would strike us as relatively form*less*. But in all of them our apprehension of prose differing with itself inclines us to intrude upon it, to do something with it that, in itself, it does not do. Its difference, then, even its continuing strangeness, is perceived as temporary. That difference is felt both as a resistance and as a weakness, or even as a vacancy to be filled.

The question now is what more specifically, and given the absence of any *presumed* "other language" with which we might replace the one we are encountering, are we looking for when we so "intrude"? If incremental differing within a verbal form makes it seem "weak," what sort of "strength" will alleviate that condition? If the effort to "understand" an expression—in Wittgenstein's terms—by replacing it with another is often begun without knowing exactly what that "other" might be, what verbal form will satisfy the search? These questions may in part be answered by looking at another example from Hemingway, but of a structure quite different from the one I have considered. It is a grammar that seems to do for itself what otherwise a reader might be trying to do: "We ate the sandwiches and drank the Chablis and watched the country out of the window. The grain was just beginning to ripen and the fields were full of poppies. The pastureland was green, and there were fine trees, and sometimes big rivers and chateaux off in the trees" (*SAR*, 87).

At its beginning, this passage pursues the variational mode that I have described. The individual terms of the sentences are commonplace: ate and drank and watched, grain and fields and poppies. Their difference is among themselves, and it is emphasized by a grammar that is so "weak," so presentational, that it seems both to allow for anything to be said and to allow the mind's eye to move over these elements much as it would over a list of discrete items. This is, therefore, highly realistic writing; its illusion is that anything can next be said because anything can next be seen, as if one felt that the "weaker" the grammar, the more it allowed for all the facts. But what seems most "realistic" here, once again, is our imaginative motion from one increment to another, a progressive, digestive motion that seems to resemble certain sorts of nonliterary perception, seems an effort to do something with these "facts."

But the last sentence of the passage accomplishes a change: "The pastureland was green, and there were fine trees, and sometimes big rivers and chateaux off in the trees." Imaginative progress is here dramatically arrested, as if something had been concluded, as if, at least for the moment, one did not need to go on. And what seems extraordinary is the slightness of the grammatical alteration that accomplishes such a decided change of motive. The mere repetition of "trees" has made all that was new suddenly familiar, as if confirmed, or corroborated, or settled.

Hemingway sometimes achieves this effect in a more extended way, so as to preserve a balance between the unknown and the known and produce the illusion that successive grammatical differences—and the unforeseen and contingent phenomena they seem to mark—are absolutely necessary, even inevitable.

> The stretch of ground from the edge of the town to the *bull-ring* was muddy. There was a *crowd* all along the *fence* that led to the *ring*, and the outside balconies and the top of the *bull-ring* were solid with people. I heard the rocket and I knew I could not get into the *ring* in time to see the *bulls* come in, so I shoved through the *crowd* to the *fence*. I was pushed close against the planks of the *fence*. Between the two *fences* of the runway the police were clearing the *crowd*

> along. They walked or trotted on into the *bull-ring*. Then people commenced to come running. A drunk slipped and fell. Two policemen grabbed him and rushed him over to the *fence*. The *crowd* were running fast now. There was a great shout from the *crowd*. . . . (*SAR*, 196; my emphases)

The terms that I have emphasized cycle reassuringly through this passage and seem to secure what otherwise is a hectic variability. In part, this assurance seems visual. These words have to be repeated because they name reoccurring properties or parts of the scene, and acknowledging and reacknowledging them seems evidence both that this scene is real and that it is perceived honestly. But this repetition is even more markedly "aural," and the repeated elements seem much more opaque than transparent. Their regular beating through the different syntactic forms in which they are embedded, and against the phrasings that do not contain them, embodies the sequence with a rhythm, converts it to a pattern, as if while everything was changing and moving, everything was staying the same. Movement here, one might say, is stylized. In these proportions the frequencies of repetition and variation compose, again, a balance, between motion and rest. This is still, as I see it, Hemingway's "realistic" mode, but it is a unique mode—a technique and effect that, I think, he should be given credit for having invented. It is a technique that both generates and satisfies one's desire to know its sequences and redefines the novel differentiation of those sequences as already familiar, as if we knew already what we were just finding out and were at home in our explorations.

Yet to say that this is still "realism" is to say as well that "exploration" is still the motive here. The movement of the imagination may be assured and secure, and the elements of Hemingway's sequences may feel unusually solid and reliable, but in the proportions I have been describing the feeling of movement dominates the stability of the repeating terms. Something very different from this happens, however, at another repetitive frequency.

> Outside, in front of the chalet a road went up the mountain. The wheel ruts and ridges were iron hard with the frost, and the road climbed steadily through the forest and up and around the moun-

> tain to where there were meadows, and barns and cabins in the meadows at the edge of the woods looking across the valley. The valley was deep and there was a stream at the bottom that flowed down into the lake and when the wind blew across the valley you could hear the stream in the rocks. (*FTA*, 289–90)

The most obvious effect of this writing—and I hope that it seems to other readers, as it does to me, writing of remarkable beauty and power —is a certain inevitability and security, a feeling of rest. If the feeling that it gives as well is that of a perfect "picture," it is a picture in the sense rather of a complete and stable composition than of a vivid visual imagining. It seems to describe something that is utterly, wholly there.

But what is "there," I suggest, and very obviously so, are the words themselves, or certain words. The repeating terms here become emphatically "present" and, so far as a reader's action upon them is concerned, "irreplaceable," because they do not allow a reader to forget them. As the prose develops, it seems to carry certain of its elements along with it, and as it says something different, it says the same. The language as it progresses does not move away from itself, and the imagination in "following" it seems, again, almost at rest.

This is perhaps the most powerful effect, as I see it, that "repetition" can achieve in language, and I should try to account for it more literally. A few simple verbal elements cycle through varying syntactical constructions, functioning as figures against the ground of those variances. Because of the differing forms in which they are embedded, the repeating terms are *markedly* repeated, in a way that would not be felt in a more obviously repetitive pattern, such as one might find, for instance, in Gertrude Stein. At the same time, the repetition itself—the fact that these terms *are* the same—is disguised by the varying grammar, cloaked, at least momentarily, so that each repeated occurrence comes as the sort of surprise one feels at a "discovered check" in a game of chess. It is something that was there all along, but still now suddenly there. Comprehension and fullness seem achieved here with an absolute minimum of imaginative motion, which is again to say that the text feels complete. There is little or no impulse to go on from it, and certainly no sense that any paraphrase could be substituted for it. It is different from anything that we might say about it precisely because, I think, it does not differ with itself.

Another account of this grammar might be that in it one perceives the recurrence of certain words within and against their differing *employments*. As a given term shifts from one grammatical function to another, and thus takes on one use after another, it seems momentarily to yield to each employment and then to exceed it, both to accumulate and to deactivate its uses at the same time, and hence to separate itself from all its uses. The effect—and, again, it is one of remarkable power—is to isolate these repeating elements, to present them as if "in themselves," and yet with their grammatical possibilities, their roots of implication, still attached to them as both residue and potential. Words thus separated from but still containing their employments may seem magical. This is the apprehension of what I want to call "language in itself," "language as such."

If we return now to Wittgenstein's terminology, we may see that the verbal form I have just described is certainly one example of "something that is expressed only by these words in these positions." One of the reasons for this is that the "positions" in question seem so clearly differentiated. Because of the recurrence of certain terms, because these terms are themselves so identifiable, their various grammatical emplacements are evident in a way they would not otherwise be. But these varying "positions" are even more important in another way; in their relation to the repeated words, they exhibit the language rearranging itself. Thus, a reader's effort to do any such "arranging" here is preempted. He is not inclined to interfere with the language; it seems already to be doing for itself anything he might have wanted to do with it.

It should be clear now that if repetition—what I would call the "true" and effective repetition that is accomplished against a differential background—is so efficient in stabilizing a text, and arresting a reader's imaginative action over and through it, then it is repetition that one is characteristically seeking in his encounters with strange texts. The "weakness" that verbal differencing implies for us, and which inclines us to "interfere" in the ways I suggested earlier, is in the first place perceived as the absence of repetition. This seems a crudely general proposition—that the "strength" of a text is a function of how it repeats itself—only until we consider that the perception of repetition in a language—no matter how rudimentary—may be both the beginning and the foundation of the understanding that that language has its rules, rules that may seem the stronger exactly because they are not yet quite "familiar," and which both resist and render superfluous a reader's own more aggressively "translative" efforts with the text. The way a text repeats itself is the most fundamental sign that it has its own consistency, whether or not this is the consistency we might imagine for it, and we may be thus disposed toward acknowledgment rather than translation.

This verbal dynamic—in which the "strength" of repetitive resistance plays against the "weakness" of differential grammar, and by which language seems singled out from its employments even while exhibiting them—may be illuminated by considering, once more, Wittgenstein's inquiries into the "seeing of aspects": "Though—one would like to say—every word has a different character in different contexts, at the same time there is one character it always has: a single physiognomy. It looks at us" (PI, p. 181). This conception seems directly relevant to our considerations of how a word may insist upon its "character" by repetition through varying grammatical emplacements. But it will be useful to stay a moment longer with Wittgenstein's metaphor, with this notion of a word's having a "face," and to relate it to what he says more literally about seeing faces. The following example is one that I have used before, but I think that its particular application to this question of "language as such" justifies another look:

> I meet someone whom I have not seen for years; I see him clearly, but fail to know him. Suddenly I know him, I see the old face in the altered one. I believe that I should do a different portrait of him now if I could paint.
>
> Now, when I know my acquaintance in a crowd, perhaps after looking in his direction for quite a while,—is this a special sort of seeing? Is it a case of both seeing and thinking? or an amalgam of the two, as I should almost like to say?
>
> The question is: *why* does one want to say this?
>
> The very expression which is also a report of what is seen, is here a cry of recognition. (PI, pp. 197–98)

This question of how to describe the seeing of the "same" face in different ways, and our temptation to think of such "perception" as a combination of seeing and *thinking*, leads Wittgenstein, as we have seen previously, directly into the matter of seeing aspects; and what many various cases of such "seeing" consistently precipitate is this sort of observation: " 'Seeing as . . .' is not part of perception. And for that reason it is like seeing and again not like" (p. 197); it is "to *see* an object according to an *interpretation*" (p. 200). Always, too, this phenomenon seems to involve "recognition"—and, therefore, a certain "familiarity"—but a sharp, and as if different, recognition, as in the "dawning" or the "flashing" of an aspect. And perhaps it is this sort of vitality, for one thing, that may cause one to think, as Wittgenstein sometimes does despite the position he has just taken, that "seeing an aspect" *is* a kind of "perception," just because it has a liveliness that "thinking" and "interpreting" would not seem to have.

It may be obvious how these arguments about "aspects" might describe those verbal situations in which we see a word now as this, now as that, while at the same time seeing, through its repetition, that it remains "itself." But if we follow Wittgenstein a bit further, through a movement that we have already considered in a more general way, we shall discover a most specific relevance to "language as such." He says, as we noted earlier, that the "substratum of this experience [of seeing aspects] is the mastery of a technique" (PI, p. 208). This "mastery" is a knowledge of the possible uses of what one is looking at; it is an ability to make "certain applications of the figure quite freely." But in particular connection to the verbal dynamics we are considering, the knowledge of the uses of the word is *implicit*, built into its presentation within different grammatical employments. It is the shifting syntax itself that applies the "figure" of the word "quite freely." Language thus may be said here to "master" itself and to display that mastery. This explains and justifies Wittgenstein's most ambitious and dramatic conclusion about such cases: what words give under these conditions is a "picture of their life."

Now we may see that Wittgenstein's image of a word as a human face was not quite so metaphoric as we may have supposed, and that the "materiality" of language, to those who experience it, is not something abstract or hypothetical or figurative but an actually apprehended, *substantial* vitality. To see that a word may now be this, and then that, and then something else, and yet to recognize it always as the same word, and to see as well, and more importantly, that the grammatical sequence through which the word recurs is what controls and generates its power, is to recognize in language an almost living capacity. And this is why words that might otherwise appear as unanimated tools may through these processes come to seem "magical."

This feeling of life in language that has been imbued with its various inactive uses is, I believe, what leads Wittgenstein to say something that in different circumstances, as I suggested earlier, he will not say. Words *ordinarily* for him are something to be used and understood, and "understanding" is not—again, in that "ordinary" sense—an "experience." But to encounter words repeating, before one's eyes, through various possible uses is to experience them and to have, again, another sort of "understanding." I have tried to suggest the force of this "verbal experience," the power of the imagining produced when a word is disconnected from use but continues to imply or even to contain its possible uses. But it is important here to observe for different reasons what we have observed before: the distinction between this imaginatively experienced apprehension of a word and the very different process of actually using it in a more purposive and practical way. Once again, "meaning" is different from "the experience of meaning"; using words is different from perceiving a "picture of their life" and having the feeling of their use. This proposition will help us understand not only why we take various texts in the ways that we do but also the consequences of so taking them.

The use of words for purposes of ordinary understanding will preclude seeing their aspects, preclude experiencing them as embodiments of multiple understandings. "One doesn't '*take*' what one knows as the cutlery at a meal *for* cutlery" (p. 195). But the catch here, of course, is that anything at any time *may* be used as "cutlery." One may always put a word to use, regardless of how it is presented—just as one may always use an entire text, and translate it or paraphrase it to one's purposes—if one's need to do so is sufficiently insistent. There are no guarantees here. All that we can reasonably say is that it should be unlikely that one would put word forms that have been perceptibly *removed* from use back into use and turn them to singular employments and interpretations. Whether something is cutlery or not, after all, depends upon how hungry one is. Whether a text will be taken to present a "picture" of its many possible uses or be bent to a single use, by any given reader, may of course be a matter of particular needs.

But if we are trying to say something about the characteristics of texts themselves, trying to distinguish between texts that are inclined to disappear into use and subjugate themselves to meaning, texts easily replaced by an interpretation of them, as opposed to texts displayed and stabilized against a suppressed background of variously "possible" uses and interpretations, we have to suppose the existence of a "neutral" reader. And one of the capacities of such a reader, it may now be clear, will be that he already knows how to use texts, in all sorts of ways, and this knowledge itself founds the recognition of textual grammars that position themselves beyond use.

I have not begun to indicate the variety of forms that such grammars may take, and it is not my intention to do so, though I have suggested that repetition is always in play within them and that it inclines us to acknowledge their "strength" because it implies the presence in them of their own consistency. But I do want to give a few more examples of texts that seem to establish themselves as irreplaceable and untranslatable, as evocative of and yet different from and dominant over their interpretations. And these examples may clarify further what it means to recognize "rules" in a text that may be quite different from any in one's familiar possession but that nonetheless preclude any "translative" efforts.

The Comedian as the Letter C

I

The World without Imagination

Nota: man is the intelligence of his soil,
The sovereign ghost. As such, the Socrates

Of snails, musician of pears, principium
And lex. Sed quaeritur: is this same wig
Of things, this nincompated pedagogue,
Preceptor to the sea? Crispin at sea
Created, in his day, a touch of doubt.
An eye most apt in gelatines and jupes,
Berries of villages, a barber's eye,
An eye of land, of simple salad-beds,
Of honest quilts, the eye of Crispin, hung
On porpoises, instead of apricots,
And on silentious porpoises, whose snouts
Dibbled in waves that were mustachios,
Inscrutable hair in an inscrutable world.
(*WS*, 27)

At first look it would be hard to imagine language more apparently in need of "interpretation" than this. The obscurely philosophical or metaphysical quality of its titles implies that it is a puzzle to be solved. The obvious foreignness of many of its individual terms—together with our suspicion that some of them are made-up terms, false terms—is exceeded by another sort of strangeness: the extravagant strangeness of its verbal linkages and combinations; its terms do not "go" with each other.

These conditions have stimulated a strenuousness of interpretation, in literary criticism, of this poem and of others in Stevens's work, commensurate with their apparent problematicness. As I suggested earlier, the more that verbal situations function to differ within themselves, the simpler and more unilateral our attempts to interfere with them become; the more puzzling the expression, the more insistent the need for its solution, or the more its reading takes on the characteristics of a solution. And "solutions," of course, are "interpretations" that are clear by opposition to a given text, alternative to it.

I once argued that such responses to Stevens's poetry are not only not appropriate but also not necessary, and one of the bases for that contention was the notion that the form of his poetry often generates a kind of imaginative "overload," that Stevens presents us with so much difficulty, so many unpursuable lines, and often over such a duration, that we relinquish our efforts to translate him because he has exhausted our powers to do so.[1] But I am no longer comfortable with this argument.

For a text that resisted interpretation so continually, it now seems to me, would not become stable, and more clearly "itself," merely by virtue of sustaining that resistance. Because a reader would continue to think of *that* sort of resistance, one generated by internal differentiation, as *weak*. And that way of conceiving it might always resuscitate the expectation of some "solution"; when the only problem is energy, a tired or even exhausted intelligence is always rechargable. Opaqueness might therefore continue to be taken for eventual transparency; one's puzzlements might continue to produce the anticipation of their clarification; and one might continue to strain away from the language as it is given.

But in this poetry, especially when it seems most difficult, such a strain may be missing. It may already seem to a reader, in the opening lines I have quoted, that to "translate" them is to respond in the wrong way. And this suggests that what I have called a "differential overload" may not really be apprehended in that way at all. It may also seem that, although this language differs markedly from what a reader may already know, it does not seem "weak." In what, then, does its "strength" consist?

The answer, I think, lies in the regularity of the differential action here. The individual words of this text may be unfamiliar, and their local semantic relations with each other may be difficult, but they nonetheless seem to be arranged according to a set of rules. "Intelligence of his soil" is strange, to be sure, but it seems strange in the same way as "Socrates of snails," "musician of pears," "wig of things," and "preceptor to the sea." And this is not as "primitive" a recognition, nor as "general" a sort of grammatical perception, as one might think; for it is not only the repeated form of noun-preposition-noun that is regular here but also the similarity of all the former nouns to each other, and the consistency of all the latter nouns among themselves.

A somewhat different but even more insistent pattern may be observed in the second sentence of the passage, which begins with "An eye," cycles through six or so variations unintelligible in themselves but obviously repetitive in form, and then solidifies itself retroactively with "the eye of Crispin," which resonates both with all the previous "eyes" and with "Crispin at sea," and whose enlightening force here is utterly disproportionate to its laconic tone. As a result of this sort of "regularity," a reader's feeling by the time he reaches "porpoises, instead of apricots," and "silentious porpoises," may be—regardless of whether or not he knows what "silentious" means—a feeling of knowing something: he knows how the poem "goes."

The "grammatical" recognitions that we are now considering, then, may be crude ones and amount to noticing the simplest varieties of syntactic consistency, such as one prepositional phrase after another. Or they may be rather sophisticated and involve an understanding of how certain words resemble each other in particular *quality*—how "intelligence" and "Socrates" and "musician" and "wig" and "preceptor" might be seen to be similar—how words may group themselves into recognizable and unified vocabularies even while their immediate uses continue to be strange. But either way, these recognitions suggest that the text where we have them has its rules. And so one may begin to feel that he is dealing with some "language" here, and though it is a language that he does not yet understand—and so he cannot be *sure* that it is a language at all—its evident regularities incline him to suppose so.

This is of course a very different sort of "grammatical display" than we observed in Hemingway, where familiar words repeated through varying syntactical emplacements, and so enabled us to "experience" them, to "see their aspects." What is familiar here is either a matter of syntax itself or of semantic relations that seem very general, or "categorical." Therefore a reader may not be assured that this text composes a language; he may not yet know whether—as Wittgenstein says—"there is enough regularity here." But he will have begun to think there might be, and the words of this text thus may be experienced as the words of a language whose possibilities of meaning are less certain, and more mysterious, than those of a "language" whose exposure seems more familiar.

But they are possibilities of meaning nonetheless. And the display of the grammar in which they reside, though it may not be our language, may still be one, which is to say that we may suppose merely that it is not our language yet. Such texts as this, in other words, establish a certain integrity by exhibiting what appear to be the rules of a language; they seem sufficiently "regular" within themselves to generate our supposition that they may be *other* languages, thus far unfamiliar to us. And if that supposition seems, from this distance, weakly founded, it is nonetheless very powerful. For it is a license for this putative grammar to continue doing what it does, and it causes a reader to suspend any inclination to interfere with its progress, any attempt to translate it, at least until more of its "regularity" has been observed.

That fuller observation may or may not happen in such texts. In "The Comedian as the Letter C," in my view, it does not; or it does not happen sufficiently to make translation, or "understanding" of an ordinary sort, possible. But that does not matter, for the great trick has already been accomplished. A reader, however provisionally, has acknowledged the text as a possible "other language," and its long continuance—its sustained demonstration of its own consistencies—enforces that conception regardless of any achieved understanding.

Of course, one never *knows* that a poem is another language in the obvious way that, say, Portuguese is. But the important point is that it may display itself as one, and a reader may therefore be moved to act as if it were. When he does, he is disposed to allow its continuance, and the more it continues, the more consistent its features become. This, again, is a very different imaginative dynamic from the one we observed in considering the multiple aspects of well-known verbal forms, and perhaps one would say that it is less substantial an experience of language, but it may very much feel like such an experience nonetheless: if less settled and assured, then more expectant and continuous.

Sometimes, of course, the perception that one may be dealing with some "other language," with a "grammatical display" of some sort, occurs in literary form much less eventually and within a much narrower compass than it does, characteristically, in Stevens or, for another example of that same sort, in Milton. And it is strange that such a recognition, over such a short duration, could seem no less inescapable.

Here Lies a Lady

Here lies a lady of beauty and high degree.
Of chills and fever she died, of fever and chills,

The delight of her husband, her aunt, an infant of three,
And of medicos marveling sweetly on her ills.

For either she burned, and her confident eyes would blaze,
And her fingers fly in a manner to puzzle their heads—
What was she making? Why, nothing; she sat in a maze
Of old scraps of laces, snipped into curious shreds—

Or this would pass, and the light of her fire decline
Till she lay discouraged and cold, like a thin stalk white and
  blown,
And would not open her eyes, to kisses, to wine;
The sixth of these states was her last; the cold settled down.

Sweet ladies, long may ye bloom, and toughly I hope ye may
  thole,
But was she not lucky? In flowers and lace and mourning,
In love and great honour we bade God rest her soul
After six little spaces of chill, and six of burning.

(SP, 140)

The inverted repetition in the second line inclines this poem, almost before we know it, from a description of the "lady" toward a meditation, not so much upon the lady as upon its own expression, as if that expression were bemused with itself, or devoted much more to itself than to its subject. (In this feeling that John Crowe Ransom's poetry seems more concerned with its own language than with its subjects, of course, it resembles a good deal of twentieth-century poetry, but this disposition is so striking and extravagant in Ransom that I think he is better compared to Wyatt, or to his seventeenth-century progenitor, Andrew Marvell.) And this apprehension is reinforced throughout the poem in at least two ways: the attributes of this lady, the features of her image, are often, on the one hand, offered hastily, indiscriminately, even carelessly ("the delight of her husband, her aunt, an infant of three"; "and would not open her eyes to kisses, to wine"), as if these characteristics were being checked off, and did not matter much. And, on the other hand, they do *not* matter to a reader as do the much more energetically conflicting expressions of the poem, the way these expressions are engaged with each other, and a reader's inclination to engage with them.

One of the things we may characteristically do, as I shall argue later, with difficult poetic expressions is to try to hear in them a particularly recollected voice, to recognize in them some "local" grammar. But what "voice" says "medicos marveling sweetly on her ills"? It is not that this diction seems *identifiably* special, and local in that way, but that its combinations seem unique. It is not merely that it is quaint and "archaic" to enjoin the ladies to "thole," but far stranger than that—rhythmically as well as semantically and syntactically—to ask them to do this "toughly."

The difficulty in imagining a single, local, human speaker here, and the commensurate inability to place the "tone" of the poem, is reciprocal with the apprehension of the poem's language as *artifice*, but that is not to say that this language is "false," that the poem is not really saying what it means, or that it is "referring" obliquely to some language that is more "real." If that were so, then we could claim that "Here Lies a Lady" is in some way "ironic." But what or where is the irony?

> But was she not lucky? In flowers and lace and mourning,
> In love and great honour we bade God rest her soul
> After six little spaces of chill, and six of burning.
>
> (SP, 140)

Is there an obvious answer to that first question? And who could say that the regard for the lady that the poem has displayed—the very strength and strain of its complexity—was not love? The amazing and beautiful incoherence of the last line in playing prim, childish, belittling, and trivial implications against those which are insistently grim, sinister, and, at the last, even agonized does not allow one to establish the kind of conceptual hierarchy or regularity that would make irony possible. The lady is not being mocked; nor, more important, is the language used about her subject to some other, superior discourse that would place it ironically. Anything further that a reader might say, any paraphrase he might make, would be insufficient to contain the possibilities that the poem's language already implies.

But this is not merely a question of the inadequacy of paraphrase in relation to great poetry. For that concept puts this situation far too much in the negative. The perception of the "insufficiency" or "inadequacy" of discourse about the poem other than the poem's own is indicative of the poem's adequacy to itself. If we feel that the poem "resists" restatement, we probably do not mean that it excludes certain implications, but that it already contains them. One does not settle back into the poem's own language out of frustration, because one can do nothing else, but out of the recognition that this language holds firmly in its possession whatever we might do with it. Such linguistic "self-possession" seems a consequence of apprehending the poem as "artifice." For the "grammatical exposure" here consists in our being confronted with a language that is not our language but that, in its exhibited consistency, evidently is one: a language which, in the beautiful strangeness of its expression, compellingly invites our saying.

To recognize "language as such" in a case like this, then, is to see not so much that it obviates conversion or translation—as was the case with the examples from Hemingway—but that—as with the example of Stevens's poetry—it suspends our motives for that sort of thing: that its status as a "saying" is far more attractive than what one might say in response to it. One has to try to deal with this sort of recognition rationally and discursively, but one should not therefore suppose that as it occurs it seems a matter of rationalistic alternatives, a recognition to which we have to persuade ourselves. For we may not have to be told to acknowledge languages different from our own. When it seems appropriate, we may be ready to grant that they say just what they say, and recognize that their quality as individual and integral expressions, as grammatical exhibitions, is precisely what is so seductive about them. Which may be only to say that human beings admire and value "sayings" as such, and that the difficulty in understanding—in the sense of translating—a language is never automatically a sufficient dissuasion from our wanting to say and to hear it.

But "Here Lies a Lady" has not always so obviously comprised its own, "other" language. Ransom revised some of his work at one time or another and, to my taste, every revision that I have seen is inferior to the version that preceded it, and I think also that the "critical" justifications that Ransom gives for these revisions, specifically his comments upon the eight pairings of poem and revised poem included in the third edition of his *Selected Poems*, make nothing so clear as how unaware an artist may be of what he is doing, or perhaps how "unconceptual"—or how vulnerable to discursive pressures—his sense of what he is doing may be.[2]

But I do not want to try to demonstrate here how Ransom misconceived his poetic process or even the process of poetry more generally. If I am saddened by what he did to "Blackberry Winter," whose earlier form is not included in this text and can only now be found, so far as I know, in Matthiessen's *Oxford Anthology of American Verse*, that shall have to remain my business. But the revision of "Here Lies a Lady" will be useful for the question at hand—for what it means to say that a poem may "establish a language"—and I shall quote it in full.

> Here lies a lady of beauty and high degree,
> Of chills and fever she died, of fever and chills,
> The delight of her husband, an aunt, an infant of three,
> And medicos marveling sweetly on her ills.
>
> First she was hot, and her brightest eyes would blaze
> And the speed of her flying fingers shook their heads.
> What was she making? God knows; she sat in those days
> With her newest gowns all torn, or snipt into shreds.
>
> But that would pass, and the fire of her cheeks decline
> Till she lay dishonored and wan like a rose overblown,
> And would not open her eyes, to kisses, to wine;
> The sixth of which states was final. The cold came down.
>
> Fair ladies, long may you bloom, and sweetly may thole!
> She was part lucky. With flowers and lace and mourning,
> With love and bravado, we bade God rest her soul
> After six quick turns of quaking, six of burning.
>
> (SP, 141)

Now I shall have to quote as well, though with equal regret, Ransom's remarks concerning this version of the poem, because they help to account for what he has done to it.

> The opening stanzas of *A* and B [the original version, and the revised one] are alike; in the later stanzas B is far superior. The second stanza has the lady sitting among her newest gowns and destroying them; but there may be two interpretations. She may be planning to get a new wardrobe when she has recovered from her illness. That seems at first the sign of a great lady's vanity: why is she not talking with her husband and her child? (The aunt may be hundreds of miles away.) But she must occupy herself somehow while she can; and the husband is a wealthy and busy man, who cannot attend her at all times, while her child is forbidden her bedside. The third stanza, where chill replaces fever, is almost unutterably painful; but I was most intent upon it, and managed to the best of my ability. Lines two and three are the saddest in the poem; perhaps in all my poems. Line two has her lying "dishonored and wan like a rose overblown," where the two phrases almost rime. Line three has her at the very point of death; and line four announces the ultimate fact. In stanza four the only thing the friends and relatives can do is to bring their tokens of affection to the coffin; but these are supplemented in line three with "love and bravado" when they ask God to "rest her soul." The "bravado" may seem strange; until we reflect that any prayer has that constituent, inasmuch as it is addressed to an Unknown God whose designs we cannot thwart. The final line is new and fresh after the twenty-odd years' service of the *A* line. And lines three and four together supply, I suppose, two reasons why she was "part lucky"; first because of the devotion of her loyal subjects, and then because of the brevity of her illness. (SP, 141–42)

Ransom is explicit here about his effort to make the poem less "strange," to make it a more sensible story, a sequence more justifiable in terms of psychological and moral commonplaces about human beings, as when he lays out the two—and only two—"interpretations" of the lady's behavior in the second stanza, or when he justifies the unfortunate "bravado" of the penultimate line with theological ratiocination. And throughout his summary he insists step-by-step on the poem's sequence as one conventionally logical in relation to our common expectations about human beings in "these situations." But at what cost: we cannot fail to observe the violence that has had to be done to the poem to achieve this familiarity, to provide for more ordinary intelligibility.

Not only the soft, diffident elegance is gone from the second stanza, but also the consistent peculiarity both of its diction and the lady's actions; and its sounded complexities have been turned to the simple rhythms of assertion. And perhaps it is also clear that "first she was hot"—as compared to "for either she burned"—is just ugly, as is "but that would pass" against its predecessor, or "the fire of her cheeks decline" against "the light of her fire decline." One could justify such a judgment, it seems to me, upon every change of phrasing that has been made; and one might attribute this revisionary ugliness to the fact that the poem's expressions in the second version are too simple and direct, too explanatory. At the same time, "direct" and "explanatory" also characterize, as I have suggested, certain rhythms here, rhythms that are recognizable from without the poem rather than within it. And these are felt to be bad, perhaps, even before they are identified as too "assertive," because as they attempt to uncomplicate the saying of the poem, they complicate and compromise its indigenous rhythmic consistency and transform it from a display of a strange but integral grammar into a mere extension of a more commonplace one.

This is not merely to say, then, that the second version of "Here Lies a Lady" is weak because its energies are mixed, that what is missing is the consistency of the first version, but to note the importance of the fact that the consistency lost was a strange one. The cost of the capacity to hook up what the poem says to more ordinary accounts of the experience it relates, the cost of achieving that kind of meaning, is the loss of the poem's utter difference from such accounts. It would thus seem, again, that the beauty of the first version resides in this difference, in our perception that it displays an integral language of its own. And it should be clear that our apprehension of such a demonstrated "saying" is not felt as merely hypothetical. Our "understanding" here is not of an ordinary, "translative" sort, but is much more substantial and complex than that, an understanding in which a language seems both to be irreplaceable and to contain a certain "experience."

Ransom says—in his comment on the unrevised form of "Here Lies a

Lady"—that "the second line of stanza three here is a hexameter instead of the standard pentameter of the poem, and contains a very dubious phrase, 'like a thin stalk white and blown,' which hardly describes the image of a beautiful woman in her ravage" (SP, 140). And he is absolutely right: that phrase—one of the finest in the poem—"hardly describes" anything (just as the lovely "beautiful woman in her ravage" here hardly describes anything; and one wishes that his phrasing had taken such turns in revising the poem). Instead, it contains the possibilities of all sorts of "descriptions"; it functions as the compelling motive to descriptions. It is necessary to and it generates "interpretations," then, but it is greater than they are: because it is prior to them, since it is their source, since it seems to compose an experience rather than to describe one, but also since, as a verbal expression, it seems perceptibly to deny both its paraphrases and the need for them, since they were already, so simply and compactly, provided for.

Ransom's mistaken insistence in this same remark upon his obligation to standard meter at the expense of the more extended and enervated rhythm that, to my ear, fits more precisely the poem's particular language may make it clear, as well, how completely we may apprehend a dictional consistency, and how thorough is the complicity of diction and rhythm. And this in turn may show that the poem is not perceived so fully as a "saying"—as so integral a grammar—because it is just recognized as "a poem," as if anything that conformed to any poetic rules would qualify as a "grammatical" presentation. It is not that being a poem is being a possible "other" language, or a new language, automatically, but rather that certain expressions may make use of poetic forms and principles to achieve this status. The multiple and powerful rules of poetry may be most effective in isolating a language, in making this transition to the grammatical. But a merely poetic regularity does not necessarily accomplish this.

The features of "Here Lies a Lady" that make it a "grammatical display" in the sense that I have been claiming, that establish the thorough difference of its expression, seem to me relatively obvious. And Ransom's poetry more generally is a good and characteristic case both of this extravagant sort of "language as such" and of a reader's disposition to apprehend such language as something greater than personal idiosyncracy or indulgence. Before I leave him here, however, I need to say—as I am not ever able to demonstrate fully enough for writers I admire, in these conceptually inclined discussions, how I admire them and why—how fine a poem "Here Lies a Lady" seems to me, and how fine and memorable a poet, despite the relatively small quantity of his production, and certainly despite my objections to his revisions, Ransom is.

As my last example of this imaginative act of recognizing a text as "another language," I want to take a case that occurs for the most part in prose fiction, one that seems to me especially interesting and, also, deceptive. For it is the case in which it may seem self-evident that a way of speaking is locally, personally, and "psychologically" identifiable, and therefore apparently controlled by its connections with a reader's own intelligible vocabularies from beyond the text, when in fact as a language it takes much more dominion than that. The best single example I can give of this linguistic condition is from Faulkner's *The Sound and the Fury*, Benjy's narrative:

> I could hear them talking. I went out the door and I couldn't hear them, and I went down to the gate, where the girls passed with their booksatchels. They looked at me, walking fast, with their heads turned. I tried to say, but they went on, and I went along the fence, trying to say, and they went faster. Then they were running and I came to the corner of the fence and I couldn't go any further, and I held to the fence, looking after them and trying to say. (*SF*, 59)

What Benjy is "trying to say," as we know from the rest of his section of the novel, is that he thinks he sees, or expects to see, or, more certainly, that he wants to see his sister Caddy, whom he used to meet on her way home from school; and he is trying as well to do something that he can never do, to talk to another human being. But what his "trying to say" amounts to, we also know, is a continuous, loud, and horrible bellowing. And along these same lines we know as well that Benjy now, at the age of thirty-three, is large, shambling, fat, drooling, and an "idiot." His mind slides along a continuum between when he was three years old and the present, and there is no difference, between these moments and among the ones they bracket, in the way he imagines the world. He has no sense of causal sequence, and what happens to him does so unexplainably; by the same token he cannot differentiate among all the scenes from his past that have proved most memorable to him; and his perpetual sorrow can be quieted only by his fixated objects: such as Caddy's slipper, an old cushion, flowers to decorate a make-believe grave, firelight.

But what seems most interesting is the way that Benjy's comparative incapacity, and his very vulnerability, becomes his individual capacity and power. As may be observed in the quotation I have just given, his inability to conceive of causal sequences enables him to notice a very great deal as it happens. And his more general free and fluid assimilation of separate historical episodes not only dramatizes and explains his imagination to us, but also shows us that these episodes are all related, even that they are the same. And his failures at "trying to say"—to the little girls on their way home from school, for an instance of which, later, he will be castrated and institutionalized, and to anyone else in his story—become his "saying" to a reader.

This effect depends, of course, upon Benjy's continuousness to a reader over a time; and so it is both something that can happen more generally only in novels or in long poems and something that I cannot demonstrate sufficiently here for his particular case. But what I am suggesting is that, sooner or later, a reader ceases to take Benjy's words at any discount, and the significance of his narrative ceases to depend upon one's regarding it as the language of an "idiot," when that language possesses an authority and resonance beyond that of any locally identifiable human language: "Father went to the door and looked at us again. Then the dark came back, and he stood black in the door, and then the door turned black again. Caddy held me and I could hear us all, and the darkness, and something I could smell. And then I could see the windows, where the trees were buzzing. Then the dark began to go in smooth, bright shapes, like it always does, even when Caddy says that I have been asleep" (SF, 85). That is the end of Benjy's narrative, and it is for me one of the most mysteriously and powerfully moving moments in fiction. It may be seen how his "causal" incapacity allows for a kind of repetitive strength that I have remarked in Hemingway, and that the simplicity of his language facilitates beautiful patterns of sound. These features, together with the fact that we know that Benjy's sorrows are by no means over, that they have hardly begun, contribute to the compellingness of this writing, but its power seems even more extraordinary than such an explanation would provide for.

One way to sharpen the account, and to understand the emotional force of Benjy's language, is to say that it somehow generalizes his case, and that his appeal is the appeal, and his language the words, of a "child." His vulnerability, which is equivalent to the fact that his wonderful imagining must remain frustrated and potential, his perpetual innocence that will be hurt again and again but never toughened, his simple comforts, and much more, all underwrite his image as a child. And so one might say that Benjy's text is "locally" identifiable after all, and that if it moves us it does so by connecting with what we already know about children.

Or by connecting with what we *think* we know. For what in fact do we know about such childhood? How do we know that experiences for children are so beautifully discrete and yet so synchronizable, or that a child "could hear us all," or feel that "the trees were buzzing," or that—when a child slept—"the dark began to go in smooth, bright shapes"? We do not, in fact, even know if Benjy sleeps, here or anytime, for the dark is doing what it "always does," and it is Caddy who tells him that he has been sleeping. I would suggest, then, that we do not recognize that Benjy is a "child" by extension from what we know about other children. If there is such a "recognition" here, it probably goes in the other direction: we know other children by Benjy; he sets a standard; he is *the* child. Indeed, he so moves us because probably he is somehow more a "child" than any particular child could be.

What happens as Benjy's narrative develops, I think, is rather like what Wittgenstein describes, in quite another context, when he says that "the same proposition may get treated at one time as something to test by experience, at another as a rule for testing" (OC, 15). Benjy's language ceases to be dominated by the rules of the grammars we bring to it; it becomes, for its duration, itself the dominating language. And the reason why this seems so remarkable is that it amounts, again, to a reversal of what we think we are doing with such narratives. For we at least begin by feeling that we "understand" them by placing them in some sort of comparative relation with rules and vocabularies of which we are assured; and yet, sooner or later, these narratives come to exceed such presumptions and to achieve a different kind of status. The character in question—and in *The Sound and the Fury* this is true also of Benjy's brothers, Quentin and Jason, as it is true of narrators in Nabokov, in Jean Rhys, in Ford Madox Ford, in Anthony Burgess, in Borges, in Hemingway, and in many others—becomes "right" to say what he says not because we can explain his speech "psychologically," not because we can be right about him, but because through the appeal of its sustained presence his language is transformed from a sort of "dialect" or merely local grammar into the only way of talking, into the language a reader must speak as he reads.

The power of this language—as we have seen earlier in different cases—is the power of possible meaning rather than that of meaning. But remaining with the example of Benjy's grammar a moment longer may help to define not only the force of "possible" here—to show again that we are not talking about something "hypothetical" or "vague"—but also the range of this concept: for what is "possible" in Benjy's story are not merely "meanings" but feelings themselves. One may be deeply moved by "associations" that in fact one does not have, by "felt" connections to situations—like Benjy's childlike ruminations on going to bed—that one could not be said to "recognize." One may feel even that he "remembers"—and this is a phenomenon that musical theorists describe as "virtual," or "unspecified" memory—things that, he also knows, never happened. And all sorts of sharply felt but mysteriously untraceable "experiences" of this kind appear to be entwined with the "possibilities" of *language*, to be produced by languages presented in their autonomous authority and substance, whose "life" may so compellingly seem to us to be our own.

CHAPTER THREE

Forms of Voice

> The way music speaks. Don't forget that even though a poem is framed in the language of information, it is not employed in the language-game of information.
>
> Might one not imagine someone who had never known music, and who came to us and heard someone playing a reflective piece of Chopin, being convinced that this was a language and people were merely keeping the sense secret from him? (RPP I: 888)

One of the aspects of the experience of "language as such" and of the force and richness of "grammatical displays," as we have seen, is the perception of the "materiality" of the language that composes these exhibitions. But this is more than a matter of certain languages insistently reminding us by their grammatical presentation that they are indeed languages, words isolated from use and freed to the play of their possibilities. What is "material" or even "physical" about language in these situations is somehow vital, and we have noted how Wittgenstein is disposed to draw analogies between words and human physiognomies and figures, and to suggest from time to time that language under these conditions has its "life."

But our access to that life in reading literature rarely takes the form of a visual recognition—that a word has a "face," for example. Much more often, this perception involves—as it does in the majority of Wittgenstein's accounts of it, where the analogy is to music, or to musical poetry—not the mind's eye, but the mind's ear. The presence of language exposed as language is most frequently a sounded presence, and the substance and substantialness of words is a matter of "voice."

The usefulness of this concept of voice in literary studies, however, has over the past decade or two been thrown into question, and, in part, these doubts are traceable to our notions about the literary imagination itself. For in the common estimation, this imagination has to do with seeing, with mental activity that is visual. An "image," after all, is something seen, and "the mind's eye" is a normal expression, while "the mind's ear" sounds eccentric. By the same token, our capacity for *describing*—often rather too inventively—imaginative "seeing" is much fuller than what we can muster for the experience of verbal sounds and rhythms. We are much more able to talk about what we see "in our minds" than about what we hear in them, partly, of course, because of the primitiveness of our schemes of prosody, but more largely because we do not expect very much of the sounded forms of speech. This visual bias, then, is conceived as justifiable; ignorance about "aural" imaginings is regarded not as a deficiency to be corrected but as evidence that these imaginings are either ineffably private or just illusory or, in relation to verbal meaning, rather trivial.

Such attitudes are to some extent inherited from neoclassical poetics, in which "sound" is altogether subordinated to "sense," and its effects imagined as pleasant but unnecessary gracings of an intelligibility more fundamental to language. And that conception, I suppose, may in turn be attributable to the even older prejudice that the mind is more "rational" than it is anything else. And of course contemporary critiques of, or attacks upon, the identification of verbal meaning with vocal effects have reinforced and extended the ignorance in question.

But I do not intend to argue with the theoretical cases against voice for two reasons. First, the counterevidence seems to me altogether too obvious. The perception or recognition of voice in literary expression is and has been simply a fact of many readers' lives, and in what follows I shall try to describe in detail some of the forms that this recognition may take. But the second reason, for not countering the argument, for example, that vocal effects cannot secure *meaning*, is more logical. For that argument *might* be quite correct so far as meaning is concerned and yet be irrelevant, for it is not meaning that is in question here. The "understanding" of what I have called "grammatical displays," as we have seen, is a grasp not of meaning but of a certain kind of "experience." Even if some were to grant that voice and its presence might have nothing to do with the meaning of language, few, I believe, would claim that voice was not a matter of their living experience of words. Voice may be so much involved in that experience, in fact, that describing its sources and effects, as we shall see, helps us to further define the characteristic features of our engagement with the "grammatical" exposures of our language.

But the examination of "voice" runs into another problem, precisely because the vocal effects that one wants to describe *are* a matter of experience, and some readers may have much less of this experience than others. And while it may be true that such differences in perceptual capacities can be more or less "natural," and that some readers or listeners have a better ear and some a worse one, there is also no doubt that, for some, the capacity for hearing language has been benumbed by their educations. Most students in literature courses, for instance, for most of their schoolroom life have been trained to be verbally tone-deaf. Evidently they have been required to convert the particularly sounded qualities of the words they encounter into something else, into paraphrases or translations more handy—for quick answers on tests, for example—than the words themselves. They have been so conditioned to read for "information," or "ideas," that it is very difficult to turn their attention back to actual and particular phrasings as these are given. For they seem to suppose that they are being asked, as they have been so often before, for another thing: the "idea behind it," or what the writer "is trying to say," or their own "interpretation"—in a word, for the "meaning."

That such readers are missing something is evident, and not merely from the personal testimony of those who claim to hear words better. Wittgenstein, as we have seen, likens the inability to perceive the "aspects" of images, for instance, to "the lack of a musical ear," which he connects in turn with an inability to "*experience* the meaning of a word": "For we want to ask 'What would you be missing if you did not *experi-*

ence the meaning of a word?' What would you be missing, for instance, if you did not understand the request to pronounce the word 'till' and to mean it as a verb,—or if you did not feel that a word lost its meaning and became a mere sound if it was repeated ten times over?" (PI, p. 214). One of the things you would be missing, we might be surprised to learn, is a capacity for *ordinary* meanings of especially subtle sorts; for the "experience" of a language's meaning, the knowledge of its "aspects," is often perceived in its sound, and this perception may determine how precisely we manage its meaning for ordinary purposes.

> Understanding a sentence is much more akin to understanding a theme in music than one may think. What I mean is that understanding a sentence lies nearer than one thinks to what is ordinarily called understanding a musical theme. Why is just *this* the pattern of variation in loudness and tempo? One would like to say "Because I know what it's all about." But what is it all about? I should not be able to say. In order to "explain" I could only compare it with something else which has the same rhythm (I mean the same pattern). (One says "Don't you see, this is as if a conclusion were being drawn" or "This is as it were a parenthesis," etc. How does one justify such comparisons?—There are very different kinds of justification here.) (PI, 527)

Here we must again remember that in Wittgenstein's use the concept of "understanding" is a dichotomous one, for it has to do both with our purchase upon the meaning of language—as I think it does in the foregoing passage—and with our having experiences of that meaning. Both the rhythms and the individually sounded qualities of words can and often do serve to limit or to define singular usages—though even then sound is not "subservient" to sense, but inseparable from it—and thus result in ordinary, meaningful understanding. But, as I shall try to show, the sound of speech, in a different mode of presentation, also and even more powerfully plays to that "understanding" that I have described as a "grammatical experience." (And here we might reflect that even in ordinarily meaningful sequences, any marked emphasis upon the sounds of one's words may incline them toward "grammatical" conditions as I have defined them.) In either of these connections, Wittgenstein's sensitivity to and privileging of the sounds of language is remarkable, but especially in the first one: we may be surprised that a philosopher so intent upon logical relations considers them often so implicated in language's sounded form.

To encounter similar attitudes in a poet might not be so unexpected, unless we were to discover, as we do in the poetics of Robert Frost, a conception of the role of hearing in verbal processes that is emphatically opposed to the one in which most of us have been educated.

> *The ear does it.* The ear is the only true writer and the only true reader. I have known people who could read without hearing the sentence sounds and they were the fastest readers. Eye readers we call them. They can get the meaning by glances. But they are bad readers because they miss the best part of what a good writer puts into his work. (PP, 255)

It is the assurance with which Frost reverses the priorities that is remarkable here. He is so confident of the rightful dominance of the ear that those whom we might nowadays consider the *majority* of readers are simply dismissed: "Eye readers we call them." And as his conception develops, we may see how far it is from any neoclassical notion of subordinate sounds for ruling sense, or soft decorations for hard truths.

> I am possibly the only person going who works on any but a worn out theory (principle I had better say) of versification. You see the great successes in recent poetry have been made on the assumption that the music of words was a matter of harmonised vowels and consonants. Both Swinburne and Tennyson arrived largely at effects in assonation. But they were on the wrong track or at any rate on a short track. They went the length of it. Any one else who goes that way must go after them. And that's where most are going. I alone of English writers have consciously set myself to make music out of what I may call the sound of sense. (PP, 250–51)

Upon his further elaboration, it becomes clear that this "sound of sense" is a matter neither of emotional "impression" nor of broad guesses about meaning. It is, as it would be for Wittgenstein, a quite particular property of grammar.

> A sentence is a sound in itself on which other sounds called words may be strung.
>
> You may string words together without a sentence-sound to string them on just as you may tie clothes together by the sleeves and stretch them without a clothes line between two trees, but—it is bad for the clothes.
>
> The number of words you may string on one sentence-sound is not fixed but there is always danger of overloading.
>
> The sentence-sounds are very definite entities. (This is no literary mysticism I am preaching.) They are as definite as words. It is not impossible that they could be collected in a book though I don't at present see on what system they would be catalogued.
>
> They are apprehended by the ear. They are gathered by the ear from the vernacular and brought into books. Many of them are already familiar to us in books. I think no writer invents them. The most original writer only catches them fresh from talk, where they grow spontaneously.
>
> A man is a writer if *all* his words are strung on definite recognizable sentence sounds. The voice of the imagination, the speaking voice must know certainly how to behave[,] how to posture in every sentence he offers. (PP, 253)

The source of these "sentence-sounds," then—of the "sound of sense"—is ordinary human talk, the way people speak. That is where they come from, and, as we shall see in a moment, that is how we often identify them when we encounter them in poetry: by associating them with particular and historical speaking situations, though they do not function in a poem, of course, as they have "ordinarily" before. But we should try to understand precisely the role of the "human" here, the importance of actual "speakers" relative to our perceptions of the sounds they have made. In English classes we may frequently ask students to describe or even to identify unnamed speakers in literature, and especially in poetry: "What kind of person would say something like this?

And to whom? And in what situation?" And it is that last question that seems the most important one. Urging the personal identification of some speaker—unless of course the poem in question is so specifically dramatic, as some of Frost's are, as to make that speaker a part of its story—is an attempt to enliven students' memories, to stimulate their recollections of verbal situations and sequences. In this way the image of the "speaker" is simply a metaphorical means to gain access to the speech rhythm that was actually heard, and what it was like to hear it.

This idea of the "speaker," in other words, is by no means the end of the inquiry, nor, even, is the recollection of the "speaking situation" itself because the understanding that one may want his students to have is that verbal expressions can be heard apart not only from speakers but from "situations" as well, apart from the remembered conditions of hearing, which conditions become, once one can hear the words on their own, merely their adjuncts or props. This development might seem hard to justify, but I think that is because it does not require justification. My claim here is simply that the sounded forms of language are, as Frost says, "very definite entities," "as definite as words," and as such they may prove more specifically memorable than the actual occasions and sequences in which they occurred.

But to say that the particularly sounded qualities of language may be more present to the mind than the situations that engendered them should not dispose us to think that these situations cease to be important. For the actual, experienced occasions in which definite speech sounds have been implicated become the *implications*—in that special sense—of those sounds when they are heard apart from those occasions. In this way the sounds of language are indicative of its "possible meanings," which are simply its recollected uses in lived situations.

These "implications," however, it is important again to remark, are not equivalent to "meanings." As we shall see more clearly in a moment, the sounds of sense, especially in Frost's work, are "dramatic." This means, on the one hand, that they are "dramatized," or, as it were, "cited." Though they may be traced to various ordinary speaking situations, they are isolated in the poetry—by many means—from them, and so their "meanings" are plural and possible rather than singular and actual. On the other hand, these sense sounds are "dramatic" because they are usually multiple and various as they occur in a poem; there they are in dialogue or even in conflict with each other. Indeed, the disjunctiveness of several different sounds of sense within a single poem itself operates to isolate them from any singular situation of meaning and hence establishes their presentation as displayed, or "grammatical." Disparities of sound here work the same way as conceptual disparities do in the case of metaphor, as I shall show in the following chapter. They accomplish the disconnection of their separate elements from matters of meaning and isolate and emphasize the grammatical capacity of these elements.

At the same time, however, these sounded forms of language are perceived, as I have suggested, as more "concrete" than the several possible situations and uses to which they may have been or might potentially be attached. In that way they do not seem plurally "possible" at all, and one's perception of them, and the "feeling" they give, may seem very singular indeed. And this singularity may tempt us to think of them as meanings, even though they are, or have become, both more solidly particular and less efficiently purposive than any meaning could be.

But even if this conception of the "sound of sense" seems logically justifiable, it might also seem, in part because Frost himself is personally so assured and declarative about sound's dominating importance, idiosyncratic, and hence removed from anyone else's actual apprehension of language. But I think this "sound of sense" may be a part of anyone's reading of Frost's poetry, and very much a fact of that poetry's imaginative life. This is especially so when the poetry is as conceptually complex and elusive as it can be, for then the sounds of phrases and lines, and the recognition of particular "voice postures" in them, may seem, at least initially, a reader's only vantage.

The most important vocal effects in Frost's poetry, for my purposes here, are the complicated ones where "large" and "abstract" grammatical sounds may be felt to control disparities of implication, or where more particularly sounded forms may embody and substantiate verbal complications that might otherwise be taken merely as "ambiguous" or even confused. But our readiness to apprehend these relatively sophisticated conditions is built upon a base of simpler and more obviously recognizable sound forms in the poetry. One might even say that we are trained up to complexities of aural impression—that the mind's ear is refined—by vocal effects that are, or should be, unmistakable:

> I have a mind myself . . .
>
> It wasn't Toffile:
> It wasn't anyone who could be there.
>
> . . . like one who takes
> Everything said as personal to himself.
>
> Ants are a curious race . . .
>
> What worked for them might work for you.
>
> Drink and be whole again beyond confusion.

These phrasings sound so clearly, I think, that we could give them a "character." I do not mean that everyone would necessarily identify each of them by describing the same "speaking character" in each case. If I might hear, for example, in "I have a mind myself"—in the shrill stringing out of those last two words—an old, wheezy man, pompous, preachy, dismissive, perhaps toothless, probably skinny, speaking to a younger audience who have to listen, or maybe, in a somewhat different and more cackling tone, to his cronies, that may be only my business. But what I am trying to suggest about that line and the rest that I have quoted is simply that they ring so definitely in our reading that we feel enabled, and perhaps even compelled, to give them an articulated and particular "character" of some sort, whose identification in personal or situational terms, once more, is just the readiest way to locate their places in our grammar.

More often in Frost's poetry there are voices that one would identify not so completely but perhaps more precisely by means of an adjective to describe their "tone":

> These flowery waters and these watery flowers . . .
>
> And I shall see the snow all go downhill . . .
>
> . . . only
> Someone who lived in turning to fresh tasks . . .

> Before I built a wall I'd ask to know
> What I was walling in or walling out . . .
>
> They cannot scare me with their empty spaces . . .
>
> Eyes seeking the response of eyes
> Bring out the stars, bring out the flowers . . .

Again, it would not matter much if everyone did not use the same adjective in each case, saying—for this sequence of quotations—wistful, childlike, preachy, self-righteous, bluff, and romantic. But it seems clear that a listening reader could use some such particular label for each line. I put this conditionally, as I did for the case of giving lines and phrases a "character," not because I think that every reader ought to be entitled to his own opinion regarding what should be heard, and, more important, not at all because I think we all hear language differently all the time, but because the labeling of such "tones" still amounts to a sort of "visual" identification that is at least one step removed from hearing them.

We may practice this visualizing of aural effects in a classroom, as I have already suggested, because in a number of ways that is to follow the path of least resistance. It is relatively easier when one wants a student to hear "how a line goes" to describe visually or "physically" how it might be said than to mimic its sound, and not merely because of a teacher's inhibitions. As Frost himself notes, a well-tuned capacity to hear the sounds of language isolated from the "ordinary" situations where they have fitted may not be capable of reproducing exactly what it hears: "I can hear it better than I can say it. And by oral practice I get further and further away from it" (PP, 255).

What is important about one's perception of all these relatively simple voices in Frost's poetry is that they establish a basis for more complex auditory receptions. These might involve the recollection of several different possible sounds for a single phrase. Or the sense derived from such a recollection might be at odds with the contextual inclinations of that phrase. Or a parallel phrasing, whose sound would clarify the first phrase, might be semantically or syntactically quite different from it. Of the penultimate line of "My November Guest," for instance—"But it were vain to tell her so"—Frost says, "Get away from the singsong. You must hear and recognize . . . the sentence sound that supports, No use in telling him so" (PP, 254). Thus, the main stress of the line in question is not "vain," as the meter might have it, but "tell." But what is important to note here is that the "sound that supports" comes from a grammatical structure different from that of the poetic original, but that nonetheless it gives us the right sound for it. From this we may draw a more general inference. Often when the hearing of a phrase, the proper "voice posture" for it, is in question, we may cast among cases that seem related to it in a number of different ways, following a directive such as "This is as if to say. . . ." And the sound that solves the problem may come from a source that seems grammatically—in the ordinary sense of grammar—quite unlike the phrase that it clarifies. But it should not therefore be supposed that the match is incorrect, or that our rapid shifting through possible rhythms was something approximate or arbitrary. To recognize the responsive flexibility of the auditory imagination should not be to question the preciseness of the results it usually achieves.

But the description of complex vocal dynamics in Frost's poetry may be better accomplished by considering their operation in a whole poem, one of his very best.

On a Bird Singing in Its Sleep

A bird half wakened in the lunar noon
Sang halfway through its little inborn tune.
Partly because it sang but once all night
And that from no especial bush's height,
Partly because it sang ventriloquist
And had the inspiration to desist
Almost before the prick of hostile ears,
It ventured less in peril than appears.
It could not have come down to us so far,
Through the interstices of things ajar
On the long bead chain of repeated birth,
To be a bird while we are men on earth,
If singing out of sleep and dream that way
Had made it much more easily a prey.

(PP, 122)

This poem displays one of the most prevailing relations of sound to sense in Frost, which, put simply, is the employment of strong, familiar sounds to contain and carry disparities and discords of implication: large sounds controlling smaller ones. "Lunar noon," for example, comes so easily to the ear that it even seems redundant, and I have heard some readers say that they actually heard it, momentarily, as "lunar moon." Thus, the subsequent realization of its simplest sense—the middle of the night—may seem natural as well, and the disintegrative energies of the phrase—moon against sun, night words against day words, one sort of brightness against another, and a good many more may seem contained. In a similar way the sounding likeness of "inborn" to the more usual "unborn" and "ingrown" also may cause us to feel that we know something before we do, and this confidence may cover the surprise of hearing the original, "inborn," more exactly, and even smooth its less pleasant associations.

Throughout the poem, in this way, strange phrasings are familiarized, and disparate implications joined, by analogies with more colloquial and recognizable speech rhythms. Nowhere is this more striking than in "it sang ventriloquist." On the one hand, the sense of this phrase seems awkward, and we may think that this is because it is *nonsense*; birds are not ventriloquists, after all, and furthermore we do not use nouns as adverbs. But that, I suggest, is a secondary sort of explanation to which we gravitate because of a prior difficulty in *saying* the phrase, "it sang ventriloquist"; the image seems fantastic, or even unformed, unseeable, because the phrasing of it seems something we cannot say. And yet at the same time this phrase tempts one to say it, as if it might sound "right" somehow, and this probably means that there is, somewhere in the language, an analogous rhythm that gives "it sang ventriloquist" the sound of sense. But while reading this poem in a class one time, I could not imagine what that rhythm was, and the sense of the phrase seemed in doubt, until someone, a very good reader indeed, suggested, "How about, 'ride shotgun'?"

This example discovers, among other things, how clumsy and inefficient it can be to investigate a problematically sounded grammar in a prescriptive and analytic way. The more that one asks here, "Where do we use nouns as adverbs? Where do we find this sort of syntax," the more one spins his wheels. For such questions are not accurate to the reading difficulty or to its solution where we appear to be imagining grammar in a very different and more immediate way as a particular unit of sound.

One might now want to say that this recollected rhythm and the familiarity and confidence that it produces compose an "access" to the sense of "it sang ventriloquist," that the sound enables us to get the sense. But this again seems a confusion of a "rational" and after-the-fact justification of a reading with its immediate apprehension. For when a familiar rhythm causes us to grant a phrase its occurrence, to accept an odd-looking verbal combination as a unit, or even a fusion, then we would seem already to have acknowledged its intelligibility, whether we could subsequently paraphrase it or not. If "sense" means actual translatability, then the sound of "it sang ventriloquist" is the indispensable way to some eventual paraphrase. But if "sense" means *grammatical* validity, means that "it sang ventriloquist" is recognized as part of some language, then the sound that allows this recognition is not a way to its sense. It is its sense. Familiarity of sound here is identical with grammatical legitimacy.

It is this identification of strange or complex attitudes individually by their particular sounds and the integration of these "smaller sounds" into larger and more compellingly recognized ones that give Frost's poetry its paradoxical qualities of irritating, brilliant elusiveness coupled with simple, matter-of-fact solidity, of a noncolloquial verbal excursion doubling as colloquial business as usual. Thus, the effort to deal discursively with the possibilities of meaning in a poem may be difficult. For in such an account we may, for one thing, have both to recognize and to justify how entire lines—and sometimes entire poems—may sound like their opposites. "Almost before the prick of hostile ears," for example, occurs in a logical rhythm where "*Just* before the prick of hostile ears" ought to be, and so it may momentarily be read in that comfortable way, though when it is heard more carefully it sustains, rather than assuages, anxiety. And "Had made it much more easily a prey," in its single-line finality, sounds grimly decisive and definitive—as if the bird were still very much in danger—against the beautifully mixed and attenuated grammar that precedes it. But it also sounds, as a continuation and fulfillment of that grammar, quietly and paternally reassuring.

It may be obvious that each of these alternative "grammars" for the last line is experienced as a rhythmic pattern and depends upon the set of sounds within which one hears it. And, looking backward, this seems true for previous examples as well, where all of the alternative "senses" were products of a grammatical fit that was identical with a fitting of sounded sequences of words. What this suggests, once again, is that the very idea of the "sound-sense" *relation* as a descriptive concept will not often give accurate results. For it now seems that, at least in certain cases, all the "implications" functioning in a verbal process are inseparable from particular patterns of sound.

But the justification for deemphasizing the role of "sense" in critical descriptions, or rather for denying its separability from "sound," may become clearer through another example.

The Rabbit-Hunter

Careless and still
The hunter lurks
With gun depressed,
Facing alone
The alder swamps
Ghastly snow-white.
And his hound works
In the offing there
Like one possessed,
And yelps delight
And sings and romps,
Bringing him on
The shadowy hare
For him to rend
And deal a death
That he nor it
(Nor I) have wit
To comprehend.

(PP, 152)

This is a remarkable poem. I know of no other that accomplishes so much imaginative change while appearing so spare, or that achieves a tragic emotional complication so simply. It is that spareness and simplicity which make it useful to the question at hand. For the means by which a reader's head is turned here, continually and abruptly, first in one direction, then in another and another, and despite the inconclusive "visualness" of the poem's fragmentary syntax, are obviously vocal. Even if one were to insist that the poem was nonetheless "imagistic," he would have to allow that the wholeness of the "images" was derived from and founded upon the various "stories" of which these changing rhythms seem part. Any overall composition of the experience of this rabbit hunt is resisted by these line-by-line changes, but that does not mean that the poem is "vague." Its sounds as it proceeds are separately, and clearly, recognizable to the ear, although they do not add up to one, comprehensive sound.

But if this means that we do not know enough about this rabbit hunt, it also means that all we know is what we hear. We know that "careless" and "still," at the outset, do not sound right together unless we read "*care*less" in a special way. And we know that a lurking hunter does not go with a "depressed" gun. "Facing alone/The alder swamps" signals another direction, from another story, toward sympathy for the hunter. And "ghastly" and "snow-white," unless carefully adjusted to each other, are heard to come from very different narratives. But then, as the phrasings of the poem sound individually even more clearly, their unconnectedness increases. The dutiful hound "works," but then in the impossibly seafaring and cheerful "offing," and then demonically, and then puppyish, and then as Rover in his prime. It is as if the poem jerks abruptly from fragment to fragment, each one entailing a different and entire story.

Then there is a more conspicuous development of a sort that we may have come to expect in Frost. Because we are trying to follow the hound's progress, we may think that "bringing him on" should sound like "bringing himself onto," but the latter phrase is aurally repulsive. And so the "him" that is brought "on" the "shadowy hare"—and here again we may see how decisions of sense are made, or at least attempted, on the grounds of sound—ought to be the hunter; yet the hunter seems to have been all this while stationary, or, more accurately, unheard. Thus the phrase "bringing him on" should be awkward and confusing. But it is not, because, I suggest, the sound of this phrase recalls an analogue that cuts across such difficulties, a semantically unlike but rhythmically identical construction that seems a participant in similar contexts: "serving him up." And with this grammar, which is so different from those we might have entertained, all the pieces of this moment in the poem fall into place.

What is most interesting here is that in the effort to figure the sense of "bringing him on," in the effort to hear how to say it, a reader is likely to consider other phrasings that might work—in that they sound conventionally more sensible than the original—but then to reject them because they do not sound enough like the original; and then to accept as best an analogue whose conceptual resemblance is much less obvious but which does sound just the same and might be heard in similar situations. The best rhythmic form here thus becomes the dominant grammar and takes control despite its semantic dissimilarity. And the important inference here, again, is that this is a governance of one sound over others. "Sense" functions in cases like this one only as a vacancy to be filled; it is a question to be answered by the sounded forms of language.

Because of its festal associations, "bringing him on" is perhaps the most celebratory moment in a dark poem. But its assurance decays immediately into the isolated savagery of "rend." And then, after the chanting rhythm of "deal a death," the poem shortens its stride even more, and steps to its end through increments that, because they become less and less possible to say, cause even the sound of it all to fade. Consider, for instance, the oxymoronic conjunction in "(Nor I)" of an outburst and an aside. How does one say *that*? But this final "unsayableness" may not be surprising in a poem where a reader's fruitless effort to "comprehend" has been identical with his failure to hear a comprehensive rhythm that would include all these particular and conflicting ones.

What such a reading shows, then, is not only that the act of reading may involve a continual attempt to bring established vocal forms to bear upon what has as yet not been spoken; not only that the sense of such cases is a question to be answered by sound; and not only, even, that "sense" as an issue simply vanishes when it is attended by particular and memorable rhythms of speech. For the sad sound of "The Rabbit-Hunter" may also demonstrate just how inescapable our perception of sounded verbal forms may be even when so partial and even when more continuous sense is utterly frustrated and confused, and all we have are voices that do not fit together, whose variation and conflict we apprehend as a grammatical richness that is almost unbearable.

It is the rehearing of these voices, together with the attempt to hear how they sound together in the present situation, of course, that constitutes the "possible meaning" here, *possible* meaning because it is based upon a recognized and, in part, a reenacted connection with a complex verbalized past, with many formerly experienced vocal situations or "stories." Such possible meanings may be perceived as isolated and distinct precisely because they have been torn from the whole situations in which they would be meaningful. But by virtue of their individual distinctness, as we have seen in "The Rabbit-Hunter," they may not combine, and thus their "possibleness" seems doubled, or squared; they seem even more mysteriously "full of meaning" that cannot be realized.

But this line also leads to the more general inference that vocal forms as "grammars" have always at least a double aspect. Because in our perception of them they "apply" to—or at least have been involved in—two or more cases and contexts—at least, for instance, their "original," colloquial situation and that of the poem they now inhabit—they therefore may seem something general, as if they were "rules" that we might invoke time after time to achieve individual relevances. But they are also particular and singular, not only because they have been extracted from particular experiences of speaking, but also because any present enactment of them feels just as specific, even though it may be an echo. The quality of these sounded forms in their occurrence is always clearly present; their life seems in this way individual and local; they are not apprehended on any given occasion as "general" forms or orders, even though their movement from context to context implies that status. And this is why Frost's characterization of them as "the abstract vitality of our speech" is not a paradox.

It is this "abstractness" that is most striking about Frost's "sounds of sense" as he describes them in prose, and especially by examples in which speech rhythms are already separated or isolated from the semantic properties with which they might have singular and ordinary meanings. But the "abstract" quality of the sounded forms of language is even more complicated in his poetry. For in his poems what becomes "abstract"—what has been disconnected from ordinary verbal situations—are not merely verbal rhythms but the entire sounded "quality" of expressions, something that is so composed of various, particular sorts of "grammatical" connections and implications that it is hard conceptually to define, though, at the least, this "quality" indicates all the vocabularies with which a given expression might be associated. And so this "abstraction" is not merely the disengagement of the rhythm of a phrasing, or even of its more general, sounded features, from some sensible situation, but the isolation of the *logical* relations that such properties imply; which in turn allows the "free application" of the "figure" of the expression in many directions and displays its logical capacity or power.

This should make it clearer, I think, that this "grammatical" recognition of language's sounded quality is not at all the same as what occurs when verbal sounds are simply inseparable from singular sense, or where they are singularly engaged, as in Wittgenstein's cases where "just *this*" is the aural pattern to be recognized. The sounded properties of ordinary grammar, especially in Wittgenstein's subtle consideration, may achieve such refined meanings that we may, as he does, consider their phrasing "irreplaceable." But it is not so in one crucial respect; no matter how delicate an ordinarily meaningful phrasing might be, it must still be "replaceable" in the sense that it must be paraphrasable or translatable. Indeed, this capacity for or liability to paraphrase is necessary to meaningful language; it is one of the ways of defining how such language works. But the "irreplaceableness" that words achieve in their grammatical condition occurs when they embody such particular variety of implication so symmetrically and integrally that there is simply no substituting for them. And—as we have seen in Frost's poetry—the means of this embodiment are most often the "abstracted" forms of language's sound.

This form of voice, by which recollected sounded qualities from specific and actual linguistic situations both constitute and control present complexities of sense and establish their vital grammatical capacity is the one central to Frost's poetic process. Most often what one hears in his poetry, or employs for hearing, are idiomatic cadences, voices that one might call "local" because they come from particularly recognized verbal sequences and occasions, or "colloquial" because they are both familiar and firmly established, and whose possible meanings seem vividly particular even while "abstract." But these specifically familiar "sounds of sense" are not all that one hears.

> I thought that only
> Someone who lived in turning to fresh tasks
> Could so forget his handiwork on which
> He spent himself, the labor of his ax,
> And leave it there far from a useful fireplace
> To warm the frozen swamp as best it could
> With the slow smokeless burning of decay.
> (PP, 50)

The moral approval here, just because it is so unexceptionable—for who would object to one's living to turn to "fresh tasks"—is a bit complacent and prissy; and the recourse of "to warm the frozen swamp as best it could" is perhaps slightly more pathetic and false-naive than it is ironical and cynical. "The Wood-Pile" might have ended here, amid this delicate tangle, leaving a reader in doubt as to whether or not to approve the abandonment because the world would then seem as sad, and life as lonely and unfulfilled, as it should be; and someone would have gone on from here as, perhaps, he should have. Many of Frost's poems do end like this, with our not knowing how to feel, or how to take or say an inescapable imaginative complication.

But the last line of the poem works a sudden and intense transformation. The sound of it is not merely louder and more dramatic than the wistful, doubtful "To warm the frozen swamp as best it could," but another order of sound altogether. With "the slow smokeless burning of decay" one may feel that the poem's action has been thrown entirely into another context, a much more elemental one where the woodpile *does* warm the swamp and where a strangely resonant and powerful voice pronounces it so. And we are a long way here from the matter of "turning to fresh tasks," or from the question of approving or understanding human variousness.

It would seem that the strength of this last line comes, in part, from the "sense" that the metaphor makes, but we need to be careful in figuring the kind of "sense" it is. "Of course," one might say, 'decay' is a kind of burning!" But is it? Such a phrasing seems to undercut itself in its very expression, because it is such a rare and picky way of talking; and this would mean that "decay" is of course not normally held to be a "burning" at all, and this phrase is ironic, and the poem ends bitterly. Yet that is not how this last line feels in the reading. "The slow smokeless burning of decay" seems not ironic but utterly convincing, seems an appeal to some more "essential" order of things.

We have witnessed such an appeal before in these discussions of "grammatical displays," and it is precisely "grammatical" or "logical." "Burning" and "decay," in this mode of language, are close associates, even "essentially" the same. But there remains the question of what gives us to adopt such a perspective, in opposition to the ways in which we "normally" talk? What stimulates our conversion to this purely "grammatical" reading? Once again, the answer seems to lie in an action of sound. For unlike what precedes it, the sound of this last line is not a "local" one at all; it is not a particular, actual, colloquial rhythm of speech any more than the concept that that rhythm embodies is a normally applied idea. This is to say that its sounded presence does not dominate the poem by bringing to it a clearer rhythm from some more conventional human sequence.

Of course, all sounded language is "human," even that which would not seem to issue from a human situation in an identifiably human voice. And one *has* heard this cadence at least once before, in Milton: "Him the Almighty Power/*Hurl'd headlong flaming* from th' Ethereal Sky." This does not mean, however, that one needs to know Milton to respond to it, any more than one needed to know anything prior to being struck by the phrasing in *Paradise Lost*. Perhaps it means that any phrase so thrillingly trochaic as "hurl'd headlong flaming" would be just as strong; but then why should that be so? And why, in more particular connection to the present case, does there seem such a compelling fit between a noncolloquial rhythm and a "grammatical" perception? Why is the result such a powerful magnification and depersonalization of "voice"?

Other cases of this extravagant conversion to such "pure" grammatical conditions are relatively rare in Frost, but the poetry of Wallace Stevens is full of them.

Some Friends from Pascagoula

Tell me more of the eagle, Cotton,
And you, black Sly,
Tell me how he descended
Out of the morning sky.

Describe with deepened voice
And noble imagery
His slowly-falling round
Down to the fishy sea.

Here was a sovereign sight,
Fit for a kinky clan.
Tell me again of the point
At which the flight began,

Say how his heavy wings,
Spread on the sun-bronzed air,
Turned tip and tip away,
Down to the sand, the glare

Of the pine trees edging the sand,
Dropping in sovereign rings
Out of his fiery lair.
Speak of the dazzling wings.

(*WS*, 126)

As it begins, this poem could hardly be more local; it has, in fact, the sort of double and emphatic colloquialness that seems produced when a particular voice is mocked. The contemptuous boredom of the speaker's address to his "friends" is not racist, as it might first appear, but perhaps worse than that, for it is directed not at what "Cotton" and "Sly" might be in that connection but at the phoniness of what they habitually say and believe. Thus "kinky" both assumes and exceeds a slur at physical characteristics and suggests the perverseness of their appetite for the sort of "fishy" story that the speaker commands them to tell.

Like many of the particular or local speaking situations with which Stevens begins in his poems, this one seems already exasperated and foreclosed; but, like them again, this particular grammatical decay precedes a transformation. So that by the time we reach the last line of "Some Friends from Pascagoula," the poem is speaking, unmistakably, in a very different voice, a voice that is indeed "deepened." And while we might think that this is because the phrasing in the latter half of the poem seems itself more engaged and sincere than what preceded it, that is not necessarily so; or it is so for quite another cause. "Heavy wings" and "sun-bronzed air" and "fiery lair" all sound sufficiently like clichés still to be ironic. Why, then, are they not? Why is this *really* "noble imagery," and why is "Speak of the dazzling wings" so obviously not mocking—in consonance with the way the poem began—but as if hypnotized, breathless, and open? What has turned the satirizing of a myth into its invocation?

More than anything else, it was a change of sound —"Down to the sand, the glare/Of the pine-trees edging the sand"—which is to say, a change of grammar; but not merely the substitution of one specifically identifiable, colloquial grammar for another. The repetition of "sand" here, both cloaked and more emphatically revealed by its altered syntactic function, seems the most important of the constructions that transform a sing-song satire into an incantation. And as an incantation the expression is not the embodiment, once again, of a colloquially human voice, for it does not issue from any "normal" speaking situation. We might then say that it comes instead from a very special situation, one in which myths might be chanted, in which the voice would be that of the entranced magician or priest or singer who was its issuance. But that sort of identification seems misleading because it may be still too personal. Our inclination in hearing and recognizing this sort of language, I think, is not to attribute it to a source or context that can be particularly visualized, for it seems to exceed and to cancel all such connections, as if it were a voice without a human speaker, larger than any such speaker, a voice from nowhere, as if the language were speaking itself, and exhibiting its own powerful presence as a kind of speech far beyond and again more "essential" than colloquial enactments or recognitions.

However one may abstractly know or claim, in other words, that this is after all *some* sort of "human" voice, it does not feel that way as we apprehend it. Its phrasing is not felt as another "local grammar" but as a different order of language altogether. As may now be obvious, it is an example of that purely grammatical way of speaking that both appeals to and defines the perpetual properties of language irrespective of their local realizations, and its presence is established by modes of speech that break against and through more normal grammatical forms.

The most effective and obvious of these modes is simply repetition itself, a powerfully effective repetition that occurs—as we saw in Hemingway—both within and against more normally progressive syntactic structures. This repetition not only signals in itself a development away from "ordinary" grammar to verbal relations that are at once freer and more "essentially" or indigenously "linguistic," but it also enables and realizes the uncolloquial rhythms of speech that make this development so compelling. And what may seem remarkable is that a dynamic so simple as repetition can so utterly modify entrenched and precisely articulated verbal procedures, which are conventionally satisfying and comfortable, into a grammatical perception and experience that has all unspecified language as its authority.

This is a case very different from most of those we encountered in Frost, where often dubious *poetic* rhythms came to be informed by stronger ones from more colloquial contexts; or where slighter or stranger sounds were dominated by more familiar ones. For these dynamics always involved the recognition of a grammar more local than that of the poem itself, and the control of an indistinct or fragmentary voice by a colloquially clearer or more continuous one. But what overcomes the more ordinarily recognizable grammar in Stevens's poetry, even though it is obviously and intensely a matter of heard rhythms, is most often not so much a competing grammar as something, in all local definitions, ungrammatical. This sort of development may be seen most clearly if we diverge from this poetry for a moment and return to Hemingway.

> There were mists over the river and clouds on the mountain and the trucks splashed mud on the road and the troops were muddy and wet in their capes; their rifles were wet and under their capes the two leather cartridge-boxes on the front of the belts, gray leather boxes heavy with the packs of clips of thin, long 6.5 mm. cartridges, bulged forward under the capes so that the men, passing on the road, marched as though they were six months gone with child. (*FTA*, 4)

This example is to be sure a rather blatant one; the way its advance cancels its very process of advancing is the most extravagant that I have seen anywhere. Its grammar as a narrative progress is thoroughly transformed by its insistent returning to certain words and to rhythmic prepositional constructions. And the most striking repetition of "under the capes" is not felt, therefore, as the grammatical mistake that it is, for it takes place in an order of language already established as ungrammatical, in a sequence that is wholly incantatory, or "musical." The rules that such a repetition would violate have already been suppressed, evidently just by the work of the recurring sounds cycling through a grammatical "advance" that only serves to emphasize their rhythmic return, and thus to show that as a grammar it is not functioning.

The effect in this passage may again be somewhat crude, and I do not mean to overpraise this piece of Hemingway's writing; though I wish that other moments in his work, where something similar happens with as much power and much more subtlety, were not so underestimated as they have been. But what I want to show by such an example is that in the verbal process under consideration the status of language is converted—heightened, perhaps, or magnified—and that this is accomplished by the arrest and even the cancellation of "grammar" in its form either of intelligible verbal sequence or of identifiably colloquial speech rhythms. And the means to this end, furthermore, is a repetitive verbal mode that seems primitive compared to that grammar, but also more "elemental," and that exceeds more ordinary grammars in its ability to dominate the imagination. This, of course, is not the "sound of sense," but the sound of something else entirely.

I am not sure that I should say that this effect is a "vocal" phenomenon in Hemingway. One may in his writing often hear one sort of voice—a human voice for all its flat "matter of factness"—transform into another, much more powerful, and much less human one. But it might be more accurate to say that the transformation in question is more obviously and fundamentally a matter of *verbal* sounds, that his grammar is "depersonalized" in the first place—despite the first-person narrative mode—by its silently visual concentration, and that as it is transformed its sounds may seem to have no source but the language itself, that the language itself may seem to be speaking.

We encounter such conditions often in Stevens, where words seem so visually inclined that there seems to be very little sound to them at all, as if the "voice" of a poem was if anything a quiet and "meditative" one. Against this quietness, the sounds produced by grammatical recurrences insist very strongly indeed upon the physical presence of language. Consider this example from "The Poems of Our Climate":

Clear water in a brilliant bowl,
Pink and white carnations. The light
In the room more like a snowy air,
Reflecting snow. A newly-fallen snow
At the end of winter when afternoons return.
Pink and white carnations—one desires
So much more than that. The day itself
Is simplified: a bowl of white,
Cold, a cold porcelain, low and round,
With nothing more than the carnations there.

(*WS*, 193)

Amid the clear visual simplicity, and the more complex progress of the concept of "snow," and the serious "existential" claims, the repetitions beat. And again we may see that their force is generated not merely by saying "snow" over and over but saying it in such different ways and places. The differing syntactic situations for the recurrence make it grammatically plausible, for one thing, and give it an ordinary sense, as if it were unavoidable. But they also, once again, disguise it, so that one is taken by surprise by the same thing. This and other almost equally surprising repetitive effects convert everything here to an order of sound, so that what could not be visually true may seem to be so simply by its *saying*: "nothing more than the carnations there."

The resulting general effect in the poem—as against the cruder force of the last example from Hemingway—seems a complex alternation, a weaving of visual images with "images" that are not visual at all but that seem even more solid and secure. For an even better example of this formal alternation, and of Stevens's adroitness in managing it, I want to quote another whole poem, one not often selected for anthologies and collections, but my personal favorite.

Forces, the Will & the Weather

At the time of nougats, the peer yellow
Sighed in the evening that he lived
Without ideas in a land without ideas,
The pair yellow, the peer.

It was at the time, the place, of nougats.
There the dogwoods, the white ones and the pink ones.
Bloomed in sheets, as they bloom, and the girl,
A pink girl took a white dog walking.

The dog had to walk. He had to be taken.
The girl had to hold back and lean back to hold him,
At the time of the dogwoods, handfuls thrown up
To spread colors. There was not an idea

This side of Moscow. There were anti-ideas
And counter-ideas. There was nothing one had.
    There were
No horses to ride and no one to ride them
In the woods of the dogwoods,

No large white horses. But there was the fluffy dog.

There were the sheets high up on older trees,
Seeming to be liquid as leaves made of cloud,
Shells under water. These were nougats.

It had to be right: nougats. It was a shift
Of realities, that, in which it could be wrong.
The weather was like a waiter with a tray.
One had come early to a crisp café.

(*WS*, 228–29)

Here, as we may often observe in Stevens, a finicky, pretty delicacy is balanced and deepened by the powerful effects of repetitive forms, in this case not merely single word sounds but more complex phrasings that when read in isolation may work both as specific voices and visual images but when felt as echoes dominate the poem and turn it into a kind of magical song. The dogwoods are pink and white and therefore the girl and the dog, following that sound, are pink and white as well. The realistic action of the girl's leaning back against the dog's walking, even, becomes more inevitable as an event of sound: "had to hold back and lean back to hold him." Even a reader's puzzlement—what does it mean to "live without ideas in a land without ideas"—or his amusement at jokes he does not quite get—"There was not an idea/This side of Moscow"—are familiarized and stabilized by the sounded continuance of "ideas," "anti-ideas," and "counter-ideas." It is not that these words and phrases become "thematically" more *intelligible*, for they seem to have no other context than the poem itself, where they are thematic in a musical way, and have the undoubtable identity of the necessary parts of a pattern of sound, so that "large white horses" are *present* in the poem even though there are, really, "no large white horses."

The way these sounded formulas are continually reincorporated into a sequence of advancing and at times impenetrable grammar and are occasionally relieved by new, visual glimpses that seem both striking and gratuitous—"shells under water"—gives Stevens's language a double aspect. Through the overall soundedness of the poem's form, one hears from time to time a human voice, a "sound of sense," and one sees an image. But there seems no probability of carrying those perceptions through and turning them into the poem's "meaning." That meaning, for one thing, would be at least difficult to achieve, provisional and complicated; whereas the sounded coherence of the poem is obvious and easy, and secures its elements in a way that a paraphrase of its sense could never do. And why should we go looking for a form other than the one the poem so evidently has?

But this is very much Wallace Stevens's climate. The constancy of sounded forms in his poetry, and their employment as ungrammatical structures, make the conclusion that his poetry is "musical" inevitable. His tendency seems most often to entertain more colloquial speech rhythms only in order to convert them, by repetitive and rhythmic patterns to uproot them, from the probabilities of human experience more dramatically than merely relocating them within the presentational situation of a poem would do and to implant them in "musical" conditions where the possibilities of meaning seem to exceed any experience of recognizable language. The result, and this is only a momentary paradox, is not to strip them of implication but to free them from implications of any particular sort. In such a functionally musical structure the implications of words are multiplied because they are *thoroughly* decontextualized; their grammatical frame is widened until it seems they can mean anything—even more than, in their history, they have ever meant.

At times, and this seems especially so in his longer poems, where one is urged through language that is dense and difficult by rhythmic patterns of great energy and duration, the effect seems as close to that of music as words can get. But words are words, and not musical notes, and they continue in poetry to resist musical form and perception except in the most extraordinary cases. And this is not because of our stubborn insistence upon their individual, semantic value, or because of our fixation upon dictionary meanings. It is because words for us have their home among a set of rhythms different from musical ones, among the formed sounds that we make when we are making sense, and because as we read we are always trying to discover these sounds. Our appetite for them is almost inexhaustible. So that even when the structure of a poem seems wholly given over to musical arrangements, we may still be trying to hear the sense of it.

Autumn Refrain

The skreak and skritter of evening gone
And grackles gone and sorrows of the sun,
The sorrows of sun, too, gone . . . the moon and moon,
The yellow moon of words about the nightingale
In measureless measures, not a bird for me
But the name of a bird and the name of a nameless air
I have never—shall never hear. And yet beneath
The stillness of everything gone, and being still,
Being and sitting still, something resides,
Some skreaking and skrittering residuum,
And grates these evasions of the nightingale
Though I have never—shall never hear that bird.
And the stillness is in the key, all of it is,
The stillness is all in the key of that desolate sound.

(*WS*, 160)

Even in a poetic "progress" so reflexive as this, that seems to advance only by reiterating its previously sounded properties, even in a structure that appears to owe its growth only to affinities that cut across the probabilities of "ordinary" grammar and require the range of the entire language, one may still try to hear a human voice and so discover a more local feeling. Such a voice may seem to break the surface of the poem momentarily, especially at times when new terms are introduced and before these terms have taken their repetitive parts in the poem's dominating musical order, but these voices always succumb to that order. Yet the last line of the poem sounds different. Against the hesitant and irregular meter preceding it, its handsome dactylic rhythm seems not so much a poetic regularity as a human insistence upon a personal declaration. The key word of the line—"desolate"—seems to jump out from the repetitive scheme that has covered everything else since the "grackles"—the source of that "desolate sound"—have been gone. It seems, even, to reconnect that sound to them, and thus to re-key the tone of the poem to a human situation and a human complaint.

Such reversals are relatively infrequent in Stevens, and I have not meant to suggest that more colloquial or human sounds—what we ordinarily mean by "voice"—can compete for long against the megaphone effects of more musical forms when the poet is set upon them. But the colloquial does constitute a perpetual and tenacious resistance to its musical conversion, a resistance that seems both to give what overcomes it all the more power and to promise that such transformations are temporary. Musical form in language, as compelling as it is, seems from this angle to have the exceptional force of a holiday. It is the more human and local grammars that continue to be the highest probabilities for our experience of words, and to them, sooner or later, we shall always want to come back.

Stevens has always been known as a poet concerned with poetics, a poet who liked to write about what poets, and especially himself, were doing. And his prosier pronouncements in this direction, especially in his essays and addresses, have often seemed puzzling. But no poet, in my view, was ever ultimately so clear about his own achievements, unless it was Frost. The forms of voice to which each poet is committed, as I have tried to show, are different. Frost is more inclined to what Stevens calls in the poem that follows "an imitation for the ear." But we have seen, I think, how extraordinarily complex and moving his reach to colloquial speech forms can be. And we have also seen that as human as they are, these forms are nothing inextricably personal; they do not depend upon the presence of any speaker, imagined or otherwise, but are in the language, and make up its history and its grammar. Thus, even though these forms function differently, they seem often to share the impersonality and inevitability of the other modes of speech to which Stevens most often gravitates, modes that in crossing against our sounds of sense seem beyond them, issuing not from locales of particular human feeling but from a linguistic experience that is at once wider and freer but more special, in which the almost total independence of words from application and situation seems a magical fact of their life, in which voice exceeds its more human employments.

The Creations of Sound

If the poetry of X was music,
So that it came to him of its own,
Without understanding, out of the wall

Or in the ceiling, in sounds not chosen,
Or chosen quickly, in a freedom
That was their element, we should not know

That X is an obstruction, a man
Too exactly himself, and that there are words
Better without an author, without a poet,

Or having a separate author, a different poet,
An accretion from ourselves, intelligent
Beyond intelligence, an artificial man

At a distance, a secondary expositor,
A being of sound, whom one does not approach
Through any exaggeration. From him, we collect.

Tell X that speech is not dirty silence
Clarified. It is silence made still dirtier.
It is more than an imitation for the ear.

He lacks this venerable complication.
His poems are not of the second part of life.
They do not make the visible a little hard

To see nor, reverberating, eke out the mind
On peculiar horns, themselves eked out
By the spontaneous particulars of sound.

We do not say ourselves like that in poems.
We say ourselves in syllables that rise
From the floor, rising in speech we do not speak.
(*WS*, 310–11)

The choice that Stevens seems both to make and to describe here is not, as I see it, a choice between the two forms of voice that I have been considering. For the alternative that he rejects is too narrowly personal and intentional to be an adequate measure of the "sounds of sense." Which is to say that we know, from reading Stevens and Frost, that "X" could not be Frost. And we know as well that, no matter how particularly grounded in human experience, Frost's forms of sound may be perceived just as "abstractly" inevitable as the less sensible ones to which Stevens is committed. But still those latter sounds *are* special, and they generate from their more musical expression the more openly powerful feelings. And although both of these forms of voice may seem as established and inescapable as "words without an author," it is likely that only the one for which Stevens declares feels so utterly depersonalized, "speech we do not speak." Both forms, however, are indigenous to our language, and one might say that they mark the ends of a scale of the sounded experience of that language, which, as I have tried to show, is the readiest access we have to the experience of our grammar.

The very "materiality" of sound itself—the fact that sound is something we perceive—is what more than anything else defines this experience of language as an experience. But the complicity of sounded verbal forms with meanings—their manifold implications in actual speaking situations—makes this also, as Wittgenstein says, an "experience of meaning" in which perception and "thought" seem inseparable. In the sounds of words, therefore, we encounter not only the most immediate way to experience the possibilities of our grammar but also the easiest way to understand the paradoxical combination in this experience of singular, and even simple, verbal *substance* and various, flickering, possible meanings. And this combination may seem so thorough, and its integration so complete, that it is no wonder that we so often mistake its unity for that of meaning, even while recognizing how much more vital than meaning it is.

CHAPTER FOUR

Gambling with Language: Metaphor

> Our ordinary language, which of all possible notations is the one which pervades all our life, holds our mind rigidly in one position, as it were, and in this position sometimes it feels cramped, having a desire for other positions as well. (*Blue Book*, 59)

> One could say: "Unfamiliarity is much more of an experience than familiarity." (*Brown Book*, 127)

There is a beautiful remark in Maurice Merleau-Ponty's *Consciousness and the Acquisition of Language*: "Everything occurs in language as if the mind [esprit] were constantly taking chances" (90). To say that this expression is "beautiful" is not, of course, to say that it is true, but rather that it seems true, or that one would like to think it were true. One might therefore want to entertain it for a while, to see how it might describe verbal behavior, or how it might tie in with more customary descriptions of that behavior, to see if and how it might apply. We behave this way all the time with expressions that are new to us, taking them on and trying them out, to discover how they work among our other ways of talking. And if this is to say that in doing so we are often taking chances with new expressions, then Merleau-Ponty's remark proves itself. It is an example of the process it describes. But a more extended examination of this conception that the mind takes chances with language will be useful, I think, for I shall try to show that such "gambling" with words is an inevitable consequence of the *grammatical* engagements with them that I have been describing when what is engaged are metaphors.

The remark that I have quoted occurs in Merleau-Ponty's discussion of how language is acquired, how it is learned by children. One of his most important ideas in these considerations is, I hope, well known: "language arises from the order of things and not from the order of the subject" (4). The language-learner, in this conception, is not trying to express "himself," or to master the verbal situation in any way that is obviously self-assertive and aggressive, but he is attempting to recognize that situation, to fit himself into its established continuance.

If this way of figuring a child's learning of language seems to us appropriate or even obvious, we should remember that it is quite different from, or perhaps opposite to, a more traditional one in which it is imagined that every learner somehow invents language for himself in the first place, that he somehow already has a language—as if the "self" were already a language—that he employs to learn the one that others speak. This notion, as Wittgenstein has shown, goes at least as far back as Augustine: "Augustine describes the learning of human language as if the child came into a strange country and did not understand the language of the country; that is, as if it already had a language, only not this one. Or again: as if the child could already *think*, only not yet speak. And 'think' would here mean something like 'talk to itself' " (PI, 32). It may be easy to see—largely because of the work that Wittgenstein has done—what might be wrong with such a description, to see, for one thing, that it implicates us in an infinite regress. For how did the child learn the language it already has, but by means of some even earlier language, which of course was learned by means of a still earlier one, and so on. And if at any point in this backward search we want to stop and say of one of these languages that there was none before it, that it was "inherited," for example, or "natural," then why could we not have said that in the first place and supposed that human speech needed no learning, that it was just an exfoliation of what was already there? But this and other problems in Augustine's account have not prevented it from becoming, again, the customary one. This image of the learner as the possessor of a language prior to language, and whose posture toward the language he learns is therefore translative, has been the most persuasive one for us, which makes Merleau-Ponty's contrary model all the more interesting.

He describes, in the following sequence, Jean Piaget's experiments concerning "communication between children over seven":

> According to the established text, the adult recounts a story, or explains the functioning of a mechanism (e.g., a faucet or a syringe), to one child (called the "explainer"). Then, the explainer transmits it to the second child, the "reproducer," who must reproduce for the adult what he has understood. . . .
>
> A. [*Procedures*]
> There are two procedures:
> 1. The explainer repeats his explanation once to the adult before transmitting it to the second child. (This procedure has the advantage of controlling the explanation, but there is also the disadvantage that the second explanation may not be as good, since the child is tired.)
> 2. The first child goes immediately to find the second, and then the second transmits to the adult what he has understood. . . .
>
> B. *Results*
> 1. The explanation of physical mechanisms is better understood than that of stories. With regard to the stories, the child understands the adult better; children understand each other poorly, but express themselves well.
> 2. As to the explanation of the mechanical gadget, the phenomenon is understood better than the story, but it is not as well expressed.
> 3. In the case of gadgets, the second child understands the first one better than the first child has understood the adult in spite of the poor expression.
>
> C. *Interpretation*
> As far as the explanation of a gadget is concerned, for Piaget the best understanding comes from the fact that true communication is not in question. The second child understands the first

> one better because he had the gadget (or drawing) in front of him. He looks more at the object than he listens to the explainer. *Everything happens as if the first child believes that he has understood more than he has in reality, and as if the second child already knew in advance what the first child was explaining to him.* (57–58; my emphasis)

Because he does not conceive what happens here as "true communication," because he appears to imagine that each child is somehow remaining within himself and his own "schemes" (he remarks later that "the words which they use are only signals which awaken the schemes that the listener already possesses"), Piaget considers the children's relation to language "egocentric." But even while seeming to grant Piaget his terms, Merleau-Ponty asks for a revision.

> Do we not find the same egocentric, autistic, syncretic thinking in the adult as soon as his thinking must go beyond the domain of the acquired in order to express new notions? The notion of egocentric language can be completely modified if one admits that it exists legitimately in the adult and that it can have value for *knowledge*. In effect, a new notion cannot be explained clearly at once. The terms cannot be defined in advance since they will be fully defined only by the use that one makes of them. Consequently . . . the adult makes use of the "direct method," which consists of specifically supposing as known that which is unknown. (60)

In his supposition that "new notions" are "fully defined only by the use that one makes of them," Merleau-Ponty sounds very much like Wittgenstein, and we shall see later how this "full definition," this "use" of a new expression, both involves the "taking of chances" that he has remarked and relates to the subject of this discussion. But, for the moment, regardless of what we decide about what those children were really doing, or about what children do more generally in learning language, we may observe what appears to be similar behavior in adults when, in encountering a "new notion," they seem to be "specifically supposing as known that which is unknown." And this "supposing," in Merleau-Ponty's terms, would not seem to be "egocentric" in Piaget's sense—which is the usual sense of the concept—at all, for it is not at all obviously a matter of one's merely regarding the "new notion" as a signal for him to insist on his own "schemes."

The idea that what goes on here is "egocentric" in Piaget's way can just be dismissed, I think, if we allow for another description of this sort of behavior in both children and adults, if we consider that someone who seems to be behaving "as if he knows" might just as well be understood to be acting *as if something is known*. In this way we may see that the "knowing" posture of the listener—the "learner" of the "new notion"—need not be seen as a show of his actually knowing something but as a more responsive attitude produced by his inference that the speaker knows something, that what has just been said is a matter of some "knowledge." And this inference he draws, I suggest, from the "saying" itself, from the fact that the speaker is using what appears—for all the listener knows—to be a *language*.

This reading of the situation is at least partially supported by our everyday verbal behavior. For often when, in the attitude of such a "listener," one nods as if in agreement with or "understanding" of an at least momentarily new expression, it may not be that he "agrees" with it, in the usual sense, at all, nor that he understands what has been said in such a way as to use it himself, to make it part of his own "schemes," but simply that he has apprehended the expression as something evidently sayable and accepted it provisionally as such, preliminary to further developments. But this, of course, as I have suggested in my descriptions of "grammatical" conditions, is "agreement" of a certain kind; and it is also a certain kind of "understanding."

It might seem, along these lines, that as language users we do this sort of thing, respond this way to the expressions of other people, all the time: that we "agree" with what they say and "understand" it in the sense of entertaining it—at least temporarily, and often no more than that—without making as yet any decision about using these expressions, about trying to tie them in with vocabularies to which we are more accustomed. This kind of behavior may be characteristic of our encounters with expressions that strike us as new. And this brings us to the subject of metaphor.

The conceptual tension that Piaget discovers in his account of the children learning language—the apparent contradiction in confronting an unfamiliar expression as if one already knew something—has constituted a problem in our efforts to understand the working of metaphor ever since those efforts began. For Aristotle and most of those who took up the question after him, it was presumed that "knowledge" must be involved in the intelligible recognition of such an expression, which then generated the problem—given that the expression was in fact unfamiliar or even unrecognizable in itself—of where such knowledge was located or established. The "newness" of a metaphor, generally speaking, is expressed in the disjunctiveness, or the disparity, of the terms that it combines; these terms are at least momentarily incompatible with each other. In what, then, does their coherence consist? How do we explain it when a listener or a reader—an audience—takes these expressions as somehow "unified"? Considering what we have already observed of human tendencies in this sort of situation, it will perhaps not surprise us that such explanations have characteristically had recourse to "the mind"; and, as we shall see, we have just as much reason as we have had before to doubt that sort of accounting in the case of metaphor.

Aristotle supposed, once more, that metaphors were *based* upon "knowledge," upon conventional conceptual relations; one could understand and accept that Achilles "leapt on his foe as a lion" because one already knew that both Achilles and the lion were models or examples of "courage" (*Rhetoric*, III, 3).[1] Metaphors more generally thus merely presented something already known with an "unfamiliar air" (III, 1) and were antidotes to what was "true but dull" (III, 11). Somewhat less well-acknowledged than these propositions, however, is Aristotle's rather reluctant and quite contradictory admission that a metaphor might at times convey "a new idea, a new fact," which is not, of course, a matter of prior "knowledge" at all (III, 10). He tries to solve this problem himself by imagining that a metaphor could be both an old idea *and* a new one because the states of knowledge in a poet and his audience are different—and here is perhaps the first time that the "mind" had to play its part—a poet could already know the meaning of what he was saying while his audience did not; a "new idea" to them would be an old one for him. But of course if metaphors are always old ideas in new dress for their inventors, and for them based upon presumed conceptual relations, then they are not really "new" at all, but only apparently so to a relatively ignorant audience, and the question of a metaphor's capacity to generate actually "new facts" has been begged.

Aristotle's picture of how metaphors work—it seems fair to say—was accepted in English poetics until the eighteenth century, when it was in fullest force. But then there was a counterinsistence: metaphors, in the Romantic conception, were not merely new for their audiences but were discoveries for their creators; they constituted genuinely new knowledge and even re-created our perceptions of the world. The most famous expression of this attitude is taken to be Coleridge's celebrated distinction between "imagination" and "fancy" in the *Biographia Literaria*, for, though metaphor itself is not mentioned explicitly there, the operation of "fancy"—a capacity that operates by the "association" of previously established "fixities and definites," and from which nothing really new is known—seems to correspond to Aristotle's conception of metaphorical action, whereas "imagination"—again along lines that may seem as linguistic or grammatical for us as they were ideological or "mental" for Coleridge—"dissolves, diffuses, and dissipates, in order to recreate; or where this process is rendered impossible, yet still at all events, it struggles to idealize and to unify" (XIII).

Perhaps because we continue to see it through some such sort of Romantic lens, Aristotle's account of metaphor for us seems to describe a verbal process that is not really metaphorical at all. Empson considers, for instance, that when the conjunction of two verbal terms produces "a third more general idea which reduces them to the status of examples or illustrations," then "the metaphor as such is destroyed."[2] How much less "metaphoric" for him, then, would be a verbal combination that presumed that "third idea," where "Achilles" and "lion" did not eventually produce the idea of "courage," but were founded on it at the start.

But it is important here to note this difference: that what Aristotle imagined as in place before the fact in metaphor we nowadays conceive as coming afterward, and suppose that whatever "idea" or "knowledge" or "meaning" a metaphor might yield is just the result of treating the metaphor in a certain way after it has been expressed, in a determined effort to conceptualize it. Metaphors are presently seldom supposed to be conceptual in themselves, but to be more or less convertible to that condition. But it is also usually thought that the meaning produced by such a conversion is something less than what was somehow promised by the metaphor itself, and this has sometimes led us to imagine that there is *something* "meaningful" about metaphors that conceptual treatments of them miss. Max Black both describes this problem and may be seen to make the kind of mistake that it invites.

> Suppose that we try to state the cognitive content of an interaction metaphor in "plain language." Up to a point, we may succeed in stating a number of relevant relations between the two subjects (though in view of the extension of meaning accompanying the shift in the subsidiary subjects [*sic*] implication system, too much must not be expected of the literal paraphrase). But the set of literal statements so obtained will not have the same power to inform and enlighten as the original. For one thing, the implications, previously left for a suitable reader to educe for himself, with a nice feeling for their relative priorities and degrees of importance, are now presented explicitly as though having equal weight. The literal paraphrase inevitably says too much—and with the wrong emphasis. One of the points that I most wish to stress is that the loss in such cases is a loss of cognitive content; the relevant weakness of the literal paraphrase is not that it may be tiresomely prolix or boringly explicit (or deficient in qualities of style); it fails to be a translation because it fails to give the insight that the metaphor did.[3]

One may sympathize with several of these remarks, especially those that suggest metaphor's advantages over and losses by "paraphrase." But the problem that I have referred to is expressed in Black's location of "cognitive content" within the metaphor: not because he imagines this "content," as so many after Aristotle have done, as something prior to the construction of the metaphor, for he has said, though somewhat hesitantly, that "it would be more illuminating in some of these cases to say that the metaphor creates the similarity [the conceptual relation between its terms] than to say that it formulates some similarity antecedently existing" (MM, 37); and not because he attributes that "cognitive" power only to "similarity" and not to "disparity"; but because, more simply, it is not clear what "cognitive content" means. Its power to "enlighten" and "inform," and to provide "insight," might suggest that it is a kind of meaning, though not a "literal" one. But what kind of meaning would that be? And what kind of meaning is a "content"? Here we should remember Wittgenstein's demonstrations that meaning is located in the use or function or action of language, and is not in residence anywhere, and that to conceive it as a "content" is metaphysics. But if the "cognitive" force of metaphors in this way seems too different from "meaning" in Black's view, in another way it seems too similar. The only difference here between the "implications" of a metaphor and the "literal" statements that might be drawn from it is proportional, a problem of "emphasis" and "weight." The "literal" thus seems to differ from the "metaphoric" only in robbing the reader of the freedom to balance his own "meaning" books for himself, in its saying "too much." Despite the mysteriousness of "cognitive content," then, there seems in Black's view too little distinction between the metaphoric and the literal so far as "meaning" is concerned. There is no doubt, at least, that he considers both forms of language as *somehow* meaningful.

This perspective has fallen, more recently, into philosophical disfavor, at least for Donald Davidson, who demonstrates—in "What Metaphors Mean"—how logically it may be countered.

> The concept of metaphor as primarily a vehicle for conveying ideas, even if unusual ones, seems to me as wrong as the parent idea that a metaphor has a special meaning. I agree with the view that metaphors cannot be paraphrased, but I think this is not because metaphors say something too novel for literal expression but because there is nothing there to paraphrase. Paraphrase, whether possible or not, is appropriate to what is *said*: we try, in paraphrase, to say it another way. But if I am right, a metaphor doesn't say anything beyond its literal meaning (nor does its maker say anything, in using the metaphor, beyond the literal). This is not, of course, to

> deny that a metaphor has a point, nor that that point can be brought out by using further words.[4]

This account seems to me a severe but accurate one. For its restriction of the concept of "meaning" to the original and separate elements of the metaphoric expression both avoids philosophic confusion and emphasizes the force and integrity of these elements in the metaphoric process, as Davidson makes explicit a moment later: "Whether or not metaphor depends on new or extended meanings it certainly depends in some way on the original meanings; an adequate account of metaphor must allow that the primary or original meanings of words remain active in their metaphorical setting" (CI, 34). But as he sees it, the fact that the "original meanings of words remain active in their metaphorical setting"—which, as we shall see, is another accurate and useful notion—makes the metaphor "*patently* false." This, it seems to me, is much better than saying that the metaphor is "true," for it reminds us that it is, in the first place, a *misusage*. But it would be better still to say that metaphors are "nonsensical"—and *not* "patently" so—rather than "false," since they are grammatical misalignments rather than empirical mistakes. A somewhat similar problem arises with Davidson's remark that metaphors do not "say anything." For this seems true in a way, and yet, as I shall show, metaphorical expressions strike us very much—perhaps more than anything else—as "sayings." This suggests that we must distinguish between "saying" and "saying something," and later I shall consider how we may do this in apprehending metaphors.

Davidson's idea of a metaphor's "falseness," however, extends to another useful thought: that a metaphor does not generate a "meaning" but an "intimation," or an "effect":

> if words in metaphor bear a coded meaning, how can this meaning differ from the meaning those same words bear in the case where the metaphor *dies*—that is, when it comes to be part of the language? Why doesn't "He was burned up" as now used and meant mean exactly what the fresh metaphor once meant? Yet all that the dead metaphor means is that he was very angry—a notion not very difficult to make explicit. . . .

> There is a simple way out of the impasse. We must give up the idea that a metaphor carries a message, that it has a content or a meaning (except, of course, its literal meaning). The various theories we have been considering mistake their goal. Where they think they provide a method for deciphering an encoded content, they actually tell us (or try to tell us) something about the *effects* metaphors have on us. (CI, 45)

Although I think that he is right in suggesting that a "fresh" metaphor is not yet a "part of the language," I would stipulate that "the language" here means language used "ordinarily" or "normally," and that he is therefore still intent upon "saying about," or "saying something." For I shall want to maintain that an active metaphor very much strikes us as a language—even if not *the* language—a language much more perceptible and present than ordinary expressions are, and that this apprehension is fundamental to the strangeness and power of the metaphor's "effect."

But Davidson has made it clear, I think, that a metaphoric relation is not a conceptual one, even if "knowledge" and "meaning" may follow from a metaphor's process and especially from its deterioration as metaphor. And this conclusion that the difference between metaphors and meanings is irreducible, and that the latter can only result from the lapsing of the former, dissolves the problem about figures of speech that puzzled Aristotle most—how they can seem so radically new and still be traceable to familiar ideas and prior knowledge—simply by exploding its latter half, and denying that they can be so traced. But this may seem to leave us in a worse position than the one that Aristotle and his followers have supported with this prop of "knowledge." If the conceptual consistency of a metaphor—the "similarity" between its disparate elements, the sense of their relation—may only be produced after the fact of its expression, then on what is the metaphor "based," either in its invention or its reception? If its disjunctive parts are not somehow intelligibly appropriate to each other, then why do we talk about metaphor as a verbal form at all? What distinguishes metaphors from nonsense?

If what Davidson says about metaphors is true, furthermore—and I think much of it is—then what has prompted more speculatively inclined commentators to propose that metaphors—or figurative language more generally—do not merely have meanings but "meanings" far beyond ordinary ones, which are so "deep" that they must be associated with "myth" or "mythic thought," and located—and here is the "mind" again—in mysterious and illogical sorts of "perception."

> Two logical concepts, subsumed under the next-higher category, as their *genus proximum*, retain their distinctive characters despite the relationship into which they have been brought. In mythico-linguistic thought, however, exactly the opposite tendency prevails. Here we find in operation a law which might actually be called the law of leveling and extinction of specific differences. Every part of a whole is the whole itself; every specimen is equivalent to the entire species. The part does not merely represent the whole, or the specimen its class; they are identical with the totality to which they belong; not merely as mediating aids to reflective thought, but as genuine presences which actually contain the power, significance, and efficacy of the whole.[5]

An account of this sort may seem not only logically strained, but also self-confessedly difficult to correlate with the functioning of any language, and to depend upon other categories such as "mythico-linguistic thought." Such efforts to deal with the "synthesis" of metaphor—or of figurative usage at large—seem even characteristically to shift away from words toward some special kind of "life," toward "our actual living encounter with the world": "But the synthesis which expresses our actual living encounter with the world—the 'vitalistic synthesis'—tends to preserve the heterogeneous in its natural character (i.e. in its heterogeneity), thereby giving it a place in a meaningful whole that is not mechanical but vital. Our world thus contains an irrepressible element of paradox, of dramatic tension, and of unresolved ambiguity."[6]

This sort of accounting is of course almost avowedly metaphysical; Ernst Cassirer's "genuine presences" and Philip Wheelwright's "vitalistic synthesis" are conceptions that depend on leaving language, in its "mechanical" functioning, behind. Of course, I am not saying that what these commentators say is not "true," for to the extent that such claims *are* "metaphysical," there is no arguing with them. What is ultimately unsatisfactory about them is not that they are open to question, but that they are not. But what seems initially inefficient in these cases is that our attempts to account for the working of metaphor, our efforts to describe a *linguistic* phenomenon, have resulted in the postulation of a kind of perception and knowledge that seems beyond the capacities of language as these efforts conceive them.

Cassirer and Wheelwright, of course, are no more contending that metaphors have "meanings" than Davidson is. But they are claiming, as I think he would not, that these forms of language have much more than that, much more than meaningful language could have. And thus we ought to ask, what prompts them to talk this way, and to maintain that figurative language is an access to some unlinguistic "reality," and to describe its processes in such "vital" terms? The direction that I would take here, it may by now be obvious, is back toward language itself. I would want to answer these questions by supposing that language—though admittedly not language of the meaningful sort—need not be written out of these speculations about figurative processes, and that the mysterious perceptions and presences that one seems to apprehend in such processes are very much a matter of words: that "grammar" is the source both of the "mythic" and of the "vital" or "real" in this action of language.

To try to show how this may be true, to discover what it is about certain *verbal* behavior that has seemed to some so much a matter of "life" or "reality," and to describe that "unity" or "synthesis" in metaphor that cannot be construed as "meaning" and yet has been so readily mistaken for some form of it, I want to focus on figurative language fundamentally, in its at least initial quality as an action of words. And to do that I shall now turn to a species of metaphor as exciting and fresh, and, given its extravagant disjunctiveness, as strange and apparently difficult to explain, as any in English and American prose fiction.

The narratives of Stephen Crane are remarkably rich in figurative language, which is commensurate with Conrad's calling him the "complete impressionist," but incommensurate with his reputation as a "realist."

But, as we shall see, the dynamics of metaphor are themselves at the heart of this paradox and justify both characterizations. The first example that I want to describe is from "The Bride Comes to Yellow Sky," in which a drunken gunman is loose on the town, prowling for something to shoot, and he comes upon "the dog of the barkeeper of the Weary Gentleman Saloon," who has "not appreciated the advance of events":

> At sight of the dog, the man paused and raised his revolver humorously. At sight of the man, the dog sprang up and walked diagonally away, with a sullen head, and growling. The man yelled, and the dog broke into a gallop. As it was about to enter an alley, there was a loud noise, a whistling, and something spat the ground directly before it. The dog screamed, and, wheeling in terror, galloped headlong in a new direction. Again there was a noise, a whistling, and sand was kicked viciously before it. Fear-stricken, the dog turned and flurried like an animal in a pen. The man stood laughing, his weapons at his hips.[7]

This has always seemed to me a great moment in American fiction, and whether or not one agrees with that assessment, he may feel that its "realism" is remarkable, that this dog's behavior is absolutely right, just what one would expect of a dog in such a situation, and so on. Such feelings about realistic fiction, of course, are always suspect, for the "familiarity" upon which they seem to depend, some fit between what the prose does and what we already know, is contradicted by the surprise of the realism, by the apparent novelty of a reader's perception that seems fundamental to the realistic effect. In this particular case, the dog seems "right," I would suggest, largely because he is unfamiliar, and not like a dog at all: which is to say that his realisticness here is somehow a function of the strange phrasing that is applied to him, of metaphor.

When the dog springs up and walks diagonally away, "with a sullen head," we may feel that here at least he seems "real" by *agreement* with what has been conventionally seen and said about dogs, and not realize how richly, and metaphorically, we read that last phrase. But with "something spat the ground" and "the dog screamed," I think, something "real" is happening more evidently because nothing describable by those phrases could be, since nothing can "spit" ground and dogs are not said to "scream." And this effect becomes strongest when, "Fear-stricken, the dog turned and flurried like an animal in a pen." "Flurried" seems both improbable and exact; the "image" that it may produce seems, again, indescribable and yet unquestionable. The dog is doing something that, if any animal could do it, a bird might. But not "in a pen," or even anywhere on the earth, because the movement suggested is not simply a whirling but also a simultaneous twisting, and perhaps a sort of shaking or vibrating besides. But in such extensions one is only turning to other and weaker metaphors. The dog of the barkeeper of the Weary Gentleman Saloon seems to be doing something that no dog has ever done before. Or that no dog has ever been *said* to do before. It would appear that we think of the "new" action of a "real" dog here because the old dogs of our language do not "flurry," that we try to imagine some new "thing" that the new usage might describe; "flurried" would thus seem "physically" just right because it is linguistically just wrong.

Here the most important question in this examination of metaphor arises: why would a reader make whatever adjustment is necessary so that a new usage, a *mis*usage, might become the evidence of a "new fact"? What is the consistency of "dog" and "flurried" here, when verbally they seem so disparate, words from quite different vocabularies or local grammars? Whatever consistency it is, it seems not evidently established in the particular metaphor itself. If we observe the grammar of this passage more widely, however, we might infer that a reader has been prepared at least to expect the consistency of this strange phrase by the intermittent but continuing literal sense of the narrative and that this sense carries over onto phrasings that are more troublesome. Or we might suppose, less satisfactorily I think, that we have been primed to the expectation of sense by earlier and weaker, which is to say more conceivable, metaphors. And if we have read a good bit of Stephen Crane, we might also remember that moments of fast action in his fiction often seem the most successful moments, that the pace of his narrative sequences is important to their effects, and supports his violently figurative usage. This may be simply to say that when words seem to be moving fast we may be more tolerant of odd verbal combinations. Or it may be to suppose that at moments of strain and conflict and anticipation in his stories, his language fits by reflecting all of these qualities. This last supposition, however, seems illogical, for it presupposes a set of conditions that the words could "fit" before those conditions have been established by the words themselves. It is true that Crane's metaphors seem to work most effectively in his more exciting narrative sequences; but that is so largely because these metaphors are themselves, quite obviously, high-velocity verbal formations, which generate the very excitement that they seem to "fit."

This is most apparent when such energetic figures of speech occur in more peaceful narrative circumstances, when their conflict, and the "anticipation" that arises from it, is more markedly and merely "verbal," a matter not of continuous narrative "action" but of isolated *linguistic* behavior, so locally "linguistic" as to set aside not only the influence of our more general feelings about a narrative but also the influence of the immediate narrative context upon our efforts to "unify" or to conceptualize or simply to accept as efficient expressions that insist so stridently upon their inefficiency. To put this another way, Crane's figures often feel isolated, even in narrative place, so that citing them one by one does not misrepresent their contextual relations very much at all:

> a row of tumble-down houses leaning together like paralytics. (456)

> The cooking-stove was of course in this drawing-room, and on the fire was some kind of long-winded stew. (457)

> In a flash the company of indolent and cynical young men had vanished like a snowball disrupted by dynamite. (459)

> A wisp of smoke came from one of the windows at the end of the house and drifted quietly into the branches of a cherry-tree. Its companions followed it in slowly increasing numbers, and finally there was a current controlled by invisible banks which poured into the fruit-laden boughs of the cherry-tree. It was no more to be noted than if a troop of dim and silent gray monkeys had been climbing a grape-vine into the clouds. (461)

> The room was like a garden in the region where might be burning flowers. (464)

> He burst out then like a siphon pressed by a nervous thumb. (476)

All of these examples are from "The Monster," but that story is probably no richer a source than most of Crane's work. And, again, they stand out from their texts almost as much as they stand out in citation. Like "the blue hotel" in the story of that name, each "declares its position against any background." And what so foregrounds each verbal figure, of course, is its inappropriateness, upon which Crane seems to take every conceivable opportunity to insist. To acknowledge that his figurative usage seems so prominent is the same as to recognize that it strikes one very much as misusage. Throughout his fiction he assembles vocabularies that are remarkably unfit for each other.

Such metaphors are of course highly resistant to conceptual synthesis and are both visually and intellectually frustrating. Indeed, the more we pursue them, the more we try to fit together their parts, the more these may cease to be "parts," the more they may proclaim their separateness and individual integrity. Pressure toward likeness may thus result in more unlikeness, and often even the individual elements of the metaphor themselves may seem to grow increasingly implausible or unintelligible.

Yet every one of the metaphors that I have just quoted seems to me to function effectively as a metaphor, and in the especially "realistic" manner that Crane's metaphors usually do, despite the fact that none of them "works" in any conceptual way. Or because none of them works—for here we might consider that if these examples are successful metaphors and if the most evident characteristic of every one of them is its conventional incoherence, then it is precisely their aspect as language not working, as language out of work, that generates their effectiveness.

It may go without saying, of course, that this apprehension of language out of work is an apprehension of *language*, that because they are "conflicted," because they are examples of evident misusage, metaphors make us aware, in the first place, of their quality as "sayings," and become much more visible or audible than "working" language—some of which may surround them—would. And thus we may understand that metaphors are a type of "grammatical display," whose quality as "language as such" is established very readily by their obvious character as flagrant misusage, by their emphatic failure to function as ordinary language does.

But when we observe that such linguistic conflict or "disparity" is an easy means by which "grammatical exhibitions," as a general sort of verbal occurrence, may be produced, we should also notice in the second place that this conflict seems to give these *metaphorical* cases of such exhibitions at least one quality that seems peculiar to them: a strangely "physical" force or even "reference." Crane's metaphors—and all those similar to them in the extravagance of their disjunctiveness—are most insistently "language out of work," language that is "idling" with a vengeance. Because they are so intensely active within themselves and generate so much conceptual tension—because they seem to be "working" so hard and yet not working—they seem to be efforts in some *direction*, to be not working in relation to something beyond them and even beyond language as it conventionally stands, that is, to some quasi-physical or "quasi-real" phenomenon toward which such mixed language gropes.

I shall say more in a moment about another feature of this metaphoric process that gives it such "direction." But at this point we may see again how the "meaninglessness" of grammatical displays generates a vitality and stimulates our perception in them of some sort of "experience." We should also see, however, that in the particular case of such novel and active metaphors, the "experience" in question is quite different from what we have previously associated with the presentation of language as language. For we may remember that in describing the "experience of the meaning of a word," and in demonstrating that it depended upon a certain verbal "capability," Wittgenstein stipulated that this sort of experience was distinguishable from the experience, for instance, of having a "toothache," that logically it was a "different though related concept" of "experience" (208).

But the difference between the experience of language and other experience that is more fundamental or "direct" is not, as I think we have observed, only logical, but also phenomenological. For the "feelings" stimulated by grammatical displays are "experienced," usually and unquestionably, as *imagined* feelings; and even if it is difficult to say just what an "imagined feeling" is like, I suggest that it is obviously *unlike* actual "sensations." Yet the experience of language that *metaphorical* verbal displays produce seems much more tilted toward "actual" experience. To put this another way, the most characteristic mistake to which one is tempted with the kinds of grammatical exhibition that I have so far described is to regard them as meanings. But with metaphors—again, of the extravagant sort that we are examining here—the most characteristic mistake in our reading of them seems to occur in another direction, in which their "possible meaning" is taken much more "physically" to imply new properties or features of the perceptible world.

This is what disposes Paul de Man to suggest, I think, following Locke, that metaphors produce the imagination of the "monstrous."[8] And we may understand how this imagination depends upon the inertia of the individual vocabularies that metaphors combine. For this perpetuated conflict of languages that disengages either of them from functioning ordinarily is one of the means by which metaphors imply that they are "working" toward some future conceptualization or reference, which, because of this same conflict between its original constituents, is quite liable to seem "monstrous." But, as I mentioned a moment ago, there is another mechanism in metaphoric process that works even more efficiently to assemble its monsters, and we may begin to understand what that is by considering a remark of Paul Ricoeur's: "It is as though a change of distance between meanings occurred within a logical space. The *new* pertinence or congruence proper to a meaningful metaphoric utterance proceeds from the kind of semantic proximity which suddenly obtains between terms in spite of their distance. Things or ideas which were remote appear now as close."[9] Ricoeur is not quite clear how the change of "distance" between a metaphor's terms—the juxtaposition of two concepts which were before considered remote from each other in their applications—can amount to a change of *logical* distance, nor how an ordinarily grammatical "proximity" is "suddenly" converted into a "semantic" one, a relation between meanings. But the conception that whatever happens here must happen in "logical space," at least, makes perfect sense when we recall that in their aspect as linguistic displays, metaphors are plainly and essentially "grammatical" or "logical," and that whatever semantic affinities their heretofore separate parts may now be seen to possess arise from the fact that the associativeness of words is more manifold and free in a purely logical or grammatical atmosphere than it is in the closer air of locally applied language. But these grammatical relations, of course, are "unreal" just because they are ordinarily unjustified, and do not "apply," because they are realizable *only* within the "grammar." And yet, as Ricoeur suggests, they "appear now as close," and thus we may have to infer that a semantic proximity that is not actual—that is only grammatical in its "existence"—*appears* to be more functional because of another, more *ordinarily* grammatical sort of "proximity" that—distracted by the flash of a metaphor's disjunctiveness—we might have "assumed" or otherwise neglected to notice, that is, a crucial *syntactic* proximity. And a moment later in his discussion, Ricoeur himself seems to have assumed the importance of this feature of metaphor.

> I suggest that we call this *productive* character of the insight *predicative assimilation*. But we miss entirely its semantic role if we interpret it in terms of the old association by resemblance. A kind of mechanical attraction between mental atoms is thereby substituted for an operation homogeneous to language and to its nuclear act, the predication act. The assimilation consists precisely in *making* similar, that is, semantically proximate, the terms that the metaphorical utterance brings together. (CI, 148)

For my general purposes in these discussions Ricoeur's insistence that the "assimilation" of a metaphor's elements to each other is not mysteriously and "mechanically" "mental" is most important, for it emphasizes again that our responses to language are rooted in and determined by language itself, that the "predication act" in question does not depend upon anyone's idiosyncracies but is fundamental to language's established and largely inescapable forms. But what is most necessary to make for my immediate purposes here is the simple observation that this "predication act" is in the first place merely and actually an ordinary grammatical one, merely a matter of the "nuclear" syntactic forms that language takes in its meaningful determinations. It is by this act that more purely "grammatical" semantic associations are inclined away from their special condition and toward applied meaning; they are "*made* similar," "actively" similar in the way that has been puzzling us, by the ordinarily meaningful pressures of their syntactic situations.

Metaphors would thus seem to have a divided and a double aspect and to stimulate dichotomous and contrary motives. Their semantic conflict, on one side, foregrounds the vocabularies they combine—and generates the possibilities of meaning and the freedom of association that the grammatical condition of language allows—by throwing the meaningful sequence in which they occur, or the progressive and realistic process of a text, momentarily out of gear. But, on the other side, metaphors always contain something of this meaningful process themselves. Their syntactic shapes—X *is* Y, X *for* Y, X *is like* Y, and so on—do not support grammatical isolations, for they are the recognizable connectives of ordinary meaning and participate in those motives. And therefore metaphors may seem unlike the grammatical displays I have been considering—in which the onward movement of language upon which meaning depends is stayed by reflexive structures of various kinds—and more like *grammatical assertions* or *propositions* of some sort: grammatical exhibitions with an ostensible use, to an apparent purpose. Thus they seem to "open up" the grammar to us not purely in its undirected richness, but as if with the promise of grammatical *reform*, as if to change the way we locally, meaningfully speak at the very moment. When they do this, the illusion of "meaning" and of "realism" that they produce—especially because both may be "monstrous"—is very powerful indeed.

Which, of course, is a fine thing in fiction. But it may also be, beyond fictional limits, a very dangerous thing. I have already suggested that grammatical displays may confuse us about our linguistic capabilities, that our apprehensions of grammatical *capacities* may mislead us about what we can actually *do* with language. And it is the syntactive activeness of metaphor—of *this* variety of such displays—that stimulates us even more urgently to try them upon our ordinary experience. And this is not merely "taking chances" with words in the voluntary, playful, and quite preliminary way that seems so engaging in Merleau-Ponty's account of the children learning language, nor is it a relatively harmless entertaining of expressions because they seem "beautiful," but a "gambling" that may seem compelled in us by metaphoric language itself even when there are none of the ostensive and hypothetical, alleviating conditions of language-learning or of "aesthetic" situations, when we still suppose that we are continuing to talk of our world as conventional language has clearly established it.

It is perhaps fortunate that not all varieties of metaphor work—and give the illusion of *working*—this way. Because of the constant reach of his imagination to the most remote verbal territories, and the thorough fragmentation of his narratives—which both frustrates any settled conceptualization and sustains the need for it—and the frequent, onward rush of his narrative grammar—which is reciprocal with the moment-to-moment instability of its figurative increments—Crane's metaphors may be considered a hyperactive species of this class of grammatical display. And yet all these factors, and more, that seemed at the outset of this discussion to make his figurative usage both extravagant and difficult to explain—especially the thoroughness of its incoherence, the absence within it of the kinds of similarity or other "foundations" that have been supposed necessary to metaphoric action—may now be seen to intensify metaphors rather than to weaken them. Crane's metaphoric process thus shows us how little support of any kind, conceptual or otherwise, metaphors require in order to be metaphors, given the simple disparity of their elements and the simple syntactical modes of their combinations. His is not a special case of metaphor, then, but only an extreme one. Metaphors, stripped of their accoutrements, are as a class the most active form of "grammatical display" available to us.

Still, there are many types of metaphors in which this activeness seems diffused, or at least masked, and situations in which the coherence or consistency of disparate verbal combinations may seem the result of causes other than a forward syntactic determination toward concepts or even "realistic" identifications. In other words, there are in various other cases other reasons why a reader might accept disjunctive expressions as metaphors, reasons by which he might not be so disposed to expect a new idea or even a "new fact," and cases in which the grammatical condition would seem to be somewhat more relaxed.

For the very efficiency of metaphors in stimulating, by their semantic inconsistency, our recognition that they are "sayings"—that they are in the first place presentations of alternative languages—will often incline us, in favorable circumstances, to attribute them to an individual "sayer," and partially to discount them as the expressions of a particular, and often peculiar, human character. This is why, I believe, Aristotle shifts as if automatically from examining a metaphor to speculating, although he does not think of it as speculation, about its source, the poet. And this is also why metaphors so often seem "vocal," why they dispose us to imagine their "speakers."

A most obvious instance of this effect is the way Nabokov's metaphors work to announce someone's presence: "We passed and re-passed through the whole gamut of American roadside restaurants, from the lowly Eat with its deer head (dark trace of long tear at inner canthus), 'humorous' picture post cards of the posterior 'Kurort' type, impaled guest checks, life savers, sunglasses, adman visions of celestial sundaes, one half of a chocolate cake under glass, and several horribly experienced flies zigzagging over the sticky sugar-pour on the ignoble counter. . . ."[10] How easily those "horribly experienced flies" give us to imagine their expressive source, and to identify them with the character of one who would say something like this, and yet also prompt us to contemplate the awful prospect of "flies" with "experience." It is very much as if the verbal combination on the one hand maintained both its disparity and its cognitive force so as to produce the near-image of something monstrous, and quite "horrible," but on the other hand, as if its strange coherence was inseparable from—and isolated from any particular imagining by—Humbert's peculiar idiom, his contemptuously fastidious, nasty but ingenious ("re-passed" through restaurants; "dark trace of long tear at inner canthus") way of talking.

Often in narrative fiction, as I suggested in an earlier chapter, and very often in Nabokov, the disjunctive form of expressions may be attributed to such a "character," and verbal derangement may be apprehended as "unified," or justified, in psychological terms. At the near end of this range, Nabokov's figurative usage may be felt to cohere because so many of his narrators seem either "crazy" at the start or eventually get that way. But metaphor may stimulate us to imagine its source much more indiscriminately and widely than the recognition of a named character or narrator might entail. For its incoherence may be so extravagant as to exceed the outline of that character, no matter how "deranged," or even to exceed the limits of any possible character. In Nabokov's case, this means that his reader is always *his* reader; it is the *author's* voice that a reader seems most usually to hear, and the author's verbal performance—his display of language—that one is constantly enjoined to observe. And this suggests, as I have remarked, that we do not so much infer some "psychological" profile of the source of most "deranged" narratives as recognize him as the provider of a recognizable, consistent, and compelling set of idiomatic rhythms that are the sounds of his language.

This implies something about the perception of metaphor that is so obvious that it might seem to go without saying: that its cohering force, the motive both for making and accepting its disparate, "nonsensical" configurations as verbal units or consistencies—together with the "favorable circumstance" in which metaphors seem more isolated from application than bent toward it—is often largely a matter of sound; that what knits a semantically inappropriate expression together, and what supports its syntactic cohesiveness, is "grammar" as sounded linguistic quality. Thus, the consistency of a metaphor may be both particularly rhythmic and more generally a function of associations between the sounded features of its separate elements, associations that are all the more available because they are reciprocal with the grammatical conditions produced by this separateness.

I do not want to try to demonstrate this observation at any length here, if only for the reason that it may be at this point in my arguments self-evident; we have already seen, in my discussions of "voice," how effective both the sound forms of human grammar and more "poetic" cadences may be in controlling and containing disparate implications of all sorts. And this general verbal dynamic is so especially and locally effective in metaphors, so much a fact of their otherwise incoherent lives, that figurative usage so arhythmic, unvocal, and flat as Stephen Crane's becomes most interesting as a counterexample.

The frequent apprehension of semantic disparities as unified sounds, then, and the identification of extravagantly disjunctive expressions with the "voices" of certain characters or certain authors or, eventually, certain languages, may emphasize a metaphor's more "grammatical" presence as a display of language, and correspondingly dampen or at least delay one's eagerness to take it too vigorously in some conceptual or "realistic" direction. But this inclination toward meaning is nonetheless constitutional to metaphors, whose progressive syntactic components so sharpen and activate their displayed grammatical character that they may seem offered as "tests" of what can be said, as efforts to probe and reform how we can actually and locally speak. At the very least, then, the metaphorical forms of grammatical display might be better conceived as grammatical "illustrations"—illustrations because what they present is not only language displayed as language, as it stands for us in all of its current possibility, but a "grammatical experience" that is shaped by ordinary syntax into its most active condition, toward realistic application and relevance, and which therefore seems so rich and undetermined and yet so available and probable that we imagine it as a special kind of meaning and a special kind of life, all around us where we encounter such linguistic forms, but most compellingly "when we look into ourselves" and encounter there these "illustrated turns of speech."

CHAPTER FIVE

Saying and Imagining

"But how can the human spirit fly ahead of reality, and even *think* the unverifiable?"—Why should we not *speak* the unverifiable? For we ourselves made it unverifiable. (*RPP* 1: 827)

"But nevertheless can't I still imagine such a case?" The first thing to say is, you can *talk* about it. But that doesn't show that you have thought it through completely. (5 o'clock on the sun.) (*RPP* 2: 94)

Among the ways by which we maintain the presumption that we exceed and include the language that we speak and inhabit, we suppose that we can imagine more than we can say, that our imaginations are fuller, more active, and even clearer than our verbal means of expressing them; that in the progress from imagining to saying, something, at least, is always lost; and that, of course, some imaginings cannot be expressed at all. This is usually, to be sure, a matter of assumption rather than of assertion; we do not go around declaring it. But my guess is that most of us take for granted that the "imagination" comprehends articulable language but itself amounts to much more than that. And conversely, we suppose that anything that we *can* say, we can of course imagine.

Given the attitudes that I have already expressed in these discussions, it may come as no surprise when I propose that it is the reverse of these notions that is more likely to be true. At least I want to suggest, hypothetically, that "verbal" capacities far exceed "imaginative" ones, and that the difference between them—and the distance between them—is often a fundamentally operative feature of our verbal behavior and also a source of what most fascinates, pleases, and puzzles us about that behavior.

But how would we decide this priority between imagination and language? By "looking into ourselves" and reporting upon their relative weights, by some kind of "introspection"? Wittgenstein's answer to that question, characteristically, is not so much to deny the efficacy as to redefine the nature of such inward searching, as in the following rebuttal to one who "testifies" to his "inner" experience of words:

> "But the words, significantly uttered, have after all not only a surface, but also the dimension of depth!" After all, it just is the case that something different takes place when they are uttered significantly from when they are merely uttered.—How I express this is not the point. Whether I say that in the first case they have depth; or that something goes on in me, inside my mind, as I utter them; or that they have an atmosphere—it always comes to the same thing.
>
> "Well, if we all agree about it, won't it be true?"
>
> (I cannot accept someone else's testimony, because it is not *testimony*. It only tells me what he is *inclined* to say.) (PI, 594)

The important question in this situation, as we may know from Wittgenstein's treatment of others like it, is *why* we "incline" to say what we do. What determines the form of our remarks in such cases? And one inference that we may generally draw, not only from Wittgenstein's arguments but also from our own observations of human behavior, is that these "inward looks" are really outward, that they are appeals and responses not to what is going on inside us but to the presupposed expressive probabilities of the cases in question. In these "introspective reports," to put this more simply, what we say plays determinedly to what we suppose we ought to say—plays, therefore, to the presumed rules of the particular "introspective" situation, to the conventional implications of the concept being scrutinized. In this way, what appears to be a type of "phenomenological" inquiry—looking into oneself or at one's "internal" behavior in order to see just what one is doing, "essentially" what one is doing—is, as Wittgenstein has shown time after time in his investigations, rather a *logical* one, for what is important is what the *grammatical* probabilities allow or even urge one to conclude.

That such introspective inquiries are characteristically concerned with grammar is evident not only where specifically *verbal* "internal" behavior is in question, but also where we are interested in phenomena that are apparently unverbal, like "imaginings."

> One ought to ask, not what images are or what happens when one imagines anything, but how the word "imagination" is used. But that does not mean that I want to talk only about words. For the question as to the nature of the imagination is as much about the word "imagination" as my question is. And I am only saying that this question is not to be decided—neither for the person who does the imagining, nor for anyone else—by pointing; nor yet by a description of any process. The first question also asks for a word to be explained; but it makes us expect a wrong kind of answer. (PI, 370)

The investigation that we are now attempting, therefore, the weighing of the linguistic against the imaginative, is a grammatical investigation, an inquiry into "how the word 'imagination' is used." And it is relatively easy, as a first step, to see how Wittgenstein himself uses it.

For within his consistent effort to dispel philosophic confusions by separating particular cases of language use—particular language-games —from one another, within his overall method of grammatical description and discrimination, Wittgenstein's most frequent argumentative recourse, as may be well known, is to "imaginability." And at one point at least, he addresses himself to that practice and to the concept it involves: "There is a lack of clarity about the role of *imaginability* in our investigation. Namely about the extent to which it ensures that a proposition makes sense" (PI, 395). This remark should not be read, however, as a warning about the unreliability of "imaginability" as a criterion of "sense" when it is applied to possible expressions, but as the preamble to a stipulation by now familiar to Wittgenstein's reader: "It is no more essential to the understanding of a proposition that one should imagine anything in connexion with it, than that one should make a sketch from it" (PI, 396). When in order to determine if a proposition "makes sense" we talk about "imagining" whether or how someone might say it, we are not talking about whether he or anyone listening imagines something in order to understand it; for, once again, nothing that happens in anyone's mind is restrictive upon the meaning of language. Our concern in applying this criterion of "imaginability" is to discover whether the use of an expression itself can be imagined, if that expression can be situated within a specifically recalled, historically established form of verbal behavior or within a reasonably hypothetical extension from such a form. If it can, then we would say, following Wittgenstein, that this expression can be understood, that it does make sense in the active, functional way that we describe as "having a meaning."

It is a certain ambiguity within this concept of "to make sense," furthermore, that tells us something more about the "imaginability" of meaningful expressions. For, as one may have inferred from my previous discussions, at least one of the implications of "to make sense" is not necessarily "to be meaningful," since we have seen that "grammatical" expressions may make sense to us in all sorts of ways without possessing the fundamental characteristic of meaning, which is purposeful application. Within Wittgenstein's determined concern with language that is meaningful, "to make sense" and "to be meaningful" are usually synonymous, though there are also some cases of verbal behavior for which he grants that they cannot be. And therefore this meaningful "making sense" that imagining a use for an expression establishes is more than a matter of that expression's grammatical possibility, of its accord with general rules of grammar. For such grammatical sense must also be conceived as functional within some actual and particular speaking situation; it must have somewhere some sort of local application. "It is not every sentence-like formation that we know how to do something with, not every technique has an application in our life; and when we are tempted in philosophy to count some quite useless thing as a proposition, that is often because we have not considered its application sufficiently" (PI, 520). This capacity for application in an expression that is given as grammatically possible might be called its grammatical *probability*; it is this that we are pointing to when we say that we can imagine someone saying such and such while doing such and such, and so on. Whether or not an expression is meaningful, and "makes sense" in that active way—whether or not it is a *proposition*—is a question of its imaginableness as an expression that people might use.

This feature of the grammar of "imagination," this complicity between what is imaginable and what makes sense, does not require us to suppose, once more, that anyone who understands something must at the same time be imagining something. But if "imaginability" is so connected to actual and sensible verbal occasions, then imagining itself makes sense. The "images" in view here are pictures of language use that are taken from accomplished or accomplishable human experience, and it is thus suggested that, whether or not we have to imagine what we understand, we do understand what we imagine. And when Wittgenstein examines the grammatical implications of "imagining" in relation to one's individual experience, he appears to presume that when one has an image, that image will be intelligible in the fundamental way of being *describable*. This becomes evident when he compares the experience of a "mental image" with the "experience of meaning."

> "In both cases," we should like to say, "we are *experiencing* something, only something different. A different content is proferred—is present—to consciousness."—What is the content of the experience of imagining? The answer is a picture, or a description. And what is the content of the experience of meaning? I don't know what I am supposed to say to this.—If there is any sense in the above remark, it is that the two concepts are related like those of "red" and "blue"; and that is wrong. (PI, pp. 175–76)

The difference noted here is important; indeed, I think we shall see that this difference between the "experience of meaning" and that of "having an image" is crucial to the distinction that I am pursuing here, between *saying* and *imagining*. But for my present concern with the "content" of imagining itself what is important is the relation that Wittgenstein presumes among an "image," a "picture," and a "description." That he conceives these concepts as closely related becomes even more obvious in the next section of his arguments. "Suppose, however, that someone were to draw while he had an image or instead of having it, though it were only with his finger in the air. (This might be called 'motor imagery.') He could be asked: 'Whom does that represent?' And his answer would be decisive.—It is quite as if he had given a verbal description: and such a description can also simply take the *place* of the image." (PI, p. 177). It is no accident, of course, that "a description can also simply take the *place* of the image" in cases where "representation" of some sort is involved, in meaningful cases. Images extend by their "representation" both to "pictures" and "descriptions," and these concepts are interchangeable because they have parallel sorts of coherence and application. This connection between the proposition and the picture, of course, has been an important one in Wittgenstein's thinking since the *Tractatus*. But its comprehensiveness comes into question in his later philosophy, when he considers much more fully than before the status and action of expressions that have some but not all of the features of a "proposition," expressions that make a certain kind of "sense" but are not ordinarily meaningful. What "pictures" could be produced from them? What form would one's "imagination" of them take?

At least the beginnings of a pessimistic answer may be found in H. L. Finch's discussion of "the picture of pain as a private object," and more specifically of Wittgenstein's fantasy of turning to stone while he is in pain and of the stone's then having the pain.

> This example shows us that the whole question is tied up with the broader question of *what we can imagine and cannot imagine* and that this, in turn, is connected with the question of how even imagining makes sense. Wittgenstein points out how mere word-play may generate all kinds of images without these images having any use at all (PI, 351). We might, for example, imagine a mouse writing a sonnet, or a number (numeral) having feelings (as in movie cartoons), but from such "imaginings" nothing at all could be inferred about mice or numbers if these words are to retain their usual meanings. . . . Similarly it is of no interest to the understanding of language or the world whether we can "merely imagine" anything such as, for example, "green ideas sleeping furiously."

> All this comes under the heading of what Wittgenstein calls "image-mongery" . . . .[1]

Finch's development here of the notion that "even imagining makes sense," however, probably does not support it entirely; for his eventual claim is only the somewhat narrower one that *useful* imagining—the imagining which is of "interest to the understanding of language *or the world*"—must make sense. "Could one imagine a stone's having consciousness? And if anyone could do so—why should that not merely prove that such image-mongery is of no interest to us?" (PI, 390). Even if we could imagine what we cannot meaningfully say, and generate images from expressions—like a "conscious stone"—that are nonsensical, those images would not bear upon meaningful language. But I have already suggested that this argument may extend to the larger inference that imagining itself, whether for meaningful purposes or not, is tied to *prior* meaningful purposes, that a visualizable image must make not merely grammatical sense but the applied and restricted "sense" that we consider "meaningful." It must make a sense locally probable for human beings. I want both to try to show that this is true and to describe its consequences for our imaginative efforts upon expressions that are not meaningful.

For these efforts are obviously important to literary studies, and especially for an examination of those forms of literary expression that I am calling "grammatical displays." When the action of these forms causes one's concern with singular meaning or understanding to recede, or to be suppressed, then "word-play" is no longer "mere." If "a conscious stone" were to come urgently to our attention not as nonsense but as metaphor—as it does in at least one poem I know of—then the question of how we might imagine from it would certainly be of interest. In other words, if one is inquiring, as I am, into the relation of imagination to language across the entire range of both concepts, then the nature of "image-mongery," as opposed to those images that "make sense," becomes important. It is also, indeed, at times important to Wittgenstein. For it is not only obviously nonsensical or even metaphoric expressions that are "unimaginable" in a certain way, but also expressions that seem more legitimate: "Two pictures of a rose in the dark. One is quite black;

for the rose is invisible. In the other, it is painted in full detail and surrounded by black. Is one of them right, the other wrong? Don't we talk of a white rose in the dark and of a red rose in the dark? And don't we say for all that that they can't be distinguished in the dark?" (PI, 515). This would *seem* to be one case where what "makes sense"—our "talk of a white rose in the dark and a red rose in the dark"—is not at all necessarily what is imaginable. For the very fact that neither "painting" is right nor wrong indicates that the "image" from which both are produced is not visually clear. How one might paint from such a verbal expression might not be right or wrong, but there would, therefore, be something wrong if I asked you, "What do you imagine from 'a red rose in the dark'? What do you see in your mind?" and you answered, "I see a bright red rose surrounded by blackness." But that sounds, I might claim, too *much* like the imagining of a "picture," a very different sort of picture from that which might ordinarily be said to represent an "image"—as if you had imagined rather a special technique for imagining something than just that something, that "red rose in the dark."

Now we might have an argument, and you might say that your red rose on a black background is certainly an "image," to which I might rejoin that it is not an image of "a red rose in the dark," and so on. I do not want to try to settle this disagreement here; but I would suggest that such controversies are likely when one talks about imagining from certain expressions that appear coherent and intelligible but whose imaginative yield is, at least, both strained and strange. "If someone says he has had an image of a shining gold ball, we shall understand him; but not if he says that the ball was hollow. But in a dream a man might see a ball and *know* it was hollow" (RPP 1: 249). Wittgenstein's distinction here between images that are imagined and those that are dreamed will prove suggestive; but for the moment I want to continue with "imagining" itself. If someone says that he has had an image of a "shining, gold, *hollow* ball," and another says that he does not understand that, the latter would probably mean that in the concept of an "image" here, as determined by "shining" and "gold," "hollow" does not fit. Although it might in other circumstances be seen that a ball was hollow, that could not be seen in this case; or, "hollow" is not a visual feature in the same way, or at the same time, as "shining" and "gold." One who claimed that it was would be claiming, as it were, to be standing in two places at once, or confusing *two* images. This not only implies a presumption that images must be singular, but it also indicates how this singularity is tightly connected to what people can actually do, to ordinary human capabilities.[2] But why would the first speaker maintain, against this reasonable grain, that he could exceed such capabilities? Or, from what did his confusion of two images arise? More generally, what gives us to think that we might "see in the mind" what we could not anywhere actually see? I think the answer will once again be found to lie not in our minds, nor in any special inner capacities, but in the grammatical features of our language.

For it would appear that the two phrases under question seem both to invite and to resist imagining, and seem therefore to possess an imaginative energy or vitality that more ordinary expressions would not have. More plainly, we may respond to them as if they were challenges to our imaginative powers. But the mere fact of any such difficulty, as we have noted before in cases where a reader works against linguistic "resistance," is not adequate to explain such an aggressive response. For what is it that makes the "challenge" here acceptable as a challenge; what makes a visual difficulty a "challenge," or encourages one to apprehend an evident resistance as a probable access?

For one thing, it seems visually encouraging that we could easily picture the smaller, or incremental, images here, the "images within the 'image,'" though these imaginable "parts" are not even parts, since there is no visualizable whole. Thus, it might be inferred that it is not the "semantic" units of these expressions that are the problem, but rather their whole, "syntactic" organization, which cannot be visualized. This notion is interesting for the way it once more connects the syntax of the imaginable with actual, human, perceptual "organizations," but it is also complicated, or tricky. This is so because what counts as a "semantic" or a "syntactic" unit is not graven in stone. If the syntactic arrangements in these cases were themselves imaginable—a white rose in a fat green vase on a high table, for example—then we might think of *them* as singular, "semantic units." Indeed, it seems likely that in our verbal behavior more generally we are continually attempting to unify fragments in this way, that we are always searching for syntactic organizations that both realize expressions in our imaginations and reduce them to elements that may function "semantically." And one aspect of that functioning is a yielding of various associative probabilities, a participation in different and larger syntactic arrangements.

Such a search is not satisfied in the cases I am considering here. But it might compellingly seem that it ought to be, for there seems to be some sort of "organization" in them; these expressions seem to compose *verbal* "wholes." Both "a red rose in the dark" and "a shining, gold, hollow ball" seem to be phrases that one might use, and seem so in two ways. They are not only coherent according to the most general grammatical rules, but they also seem strangely isolated, as if in need of a more actively useful grammar—or at least a fuller one—to complete them. If we tried to think of these fuller expressions, however, what would they be? "There is a difference between a red rose in the dark and a white one"? "Over the pawnshop door I saw three shining, gold, hollow balls"? Such completions evidently do not relieve the strangeness here. They rather emphasize ambiguity than remove it; or they make it more evident that these expressions are not descriptions of images but invitations to more complicated sorts of speculation.

This suggests two things. First, the "isolatedness" of the original phrases is not merely a function of their fragmentariness or incompleteness. Their strangely unconnected quality is produced not by their saying too little, but by their saying too much. That the shining gold ball is "hollow," and that the red rose is "in the dark," amounts in each case to a grammatical excess, which is to say a grammatical conflict, a breaking of certain linguistic rules. If either remark occurred in a conversation, we might find ourselves looking at the speaker more acutely than we had been; if they occurred on a page, then the words themselves might seem italicized, or stimulative of some more special attention. This is already enough indication, I suggest, to warrant the judgment that we are dealing here, again, with a variety of "verbal display," that the "coherence" we apprehend in these phrasings—and this is the second point that follows from the observation that they generate "speculation"—is a matter not of imaginable syntax, a syntax of applied description, but of a more abstract or logical form, which does not apply language so much as *present* it, and sets us imagining about the words themselves and their possible applications.

"Imagining" in these cases therefore means rather the entertaining of possible meanings than the seeing of images, and the "vitality" that one apprehends here is a matter of verbal rather than visual energies. We may suspect further that, even though the former appears to have been mistaken for the latter, these two sorts of experience are fundamentally at odds. Wittgenstein may be seen to support this last inference when he asks, "Is it the multiplicity of possible explanations of a meaning that lies at the bottom of our not experiencing a meaning 'in the same sense' as a visual image?" (RPP 1:261) And to show how this "multiplicity" at its highest frequencies may even preclude any sort of imaginative seeing, I want to consider a case in which the inclination to the "experience of meaning" is so thorough that a reader's impulse to visualize the parts of a fictional world is completely frustrated.

Joseph Conrad's claim in the preface to *The Nigger of the "Narcissus"* that he was "above all" trying to make his reader "see" would surely be the most notoriously failed intention in literary history if we insisted that it had unequivocally to do with visual imagining, for it is followed throughout the novelist's career by narratives that, at the least, strenuously dramatize problems of vision and intelligibility. Certainly the "visual images" most characteristic of Conrad are those of mists, veils, curtains, darkness, and the like. His locales for the important actions of his stories, furthermore, are usually remote, especially in the sense that his narrators are seldom present at them at the times of these actions. And such narrative dislocations are embodied on the verbal surfaces of his stories in rhetorical figures whose visual properties are violently disjunctive, or which combine something to see with the largest and most abstract concepts, like "evil" or "truth," and which in these and other ways insist upon the provisionalness, upon the "as if-ness," of their imaginable connections. These features of his style, I would hope, are well-known; still, a few particular passages may help to illustrate just how determined is Conrad's insistence—through narrators like Marlow—upon grammatical rather than visual presence.

> "I became in an instant as much of a pretense as the rest of the bewitched pilgrims. This simply because I had a notion it somehow would be of help to that Kurtz whom at the time I did not see—you understand. He was just a word for me. I did not see the man in the name any more than you do. Do you see him? Do you see the story? Do you see anything? It seems to me I am trying to tell you a dream—making a vain attempt, because no relation of a dream can convey the dream-sensation. . . ."[3]

It is characteristic of Marlow that he is here bordering on the "incivility" to his auditors of which they sometimes accuse him, and spreading the blame for his own inability to "see." At such moments this inability is very much conceived as a "failure." But the trouble with that conception, once more, is its conflict with one's recognition that this failure is designed and built into Conrad's prose. Those readers who say jokingly that the "fog" that narrators like Marlow are trying to penetrate is generated by or even inseparable from their own turns of speech and imaginative interests are of course quite right; these narrators "fail" to see because they are in fact much more interested in doing something else, even at those moments in a story when a reader's seeing, and the singular understanding that might accompany it, would seem dramatically most necessary, as at the moment of Kurtz's death and his famous outcry.

> "It was as though a veil had been rent. I saw on that ivory face the expression of sombre pride, or ruthless power, of craven terror—of an intense and hopeless despair. Did he live his life again in every detail of desire, temptation, and surrender during that supreme moment of complete knowledge? He cried out in a whisper at some image, at some vision—he cried out twice, a cry that was no more than a breath—
>
> " 'The horror! The horror!'
>
> "I blew the candle out and left the cabin." (149)

"As though a veil had been rent." But not really, for when it is "rent" what one encounters is a combination of facial "expressions" that are unvisualizable both because their features—with the interesting and *metaphoric* exception, perhaps, of "ivory"—are abstract and "moral" and because even these "descriptive" terms multiply so freely. These expressions then precipitate a gratuitous and unanswerable question, and then a "knowledge" altogether too "complete" to be specified, and then, penultimately, "some image . . . some vision," which Marlow presumes that Kurtz has but is unavailable to him and to us, whose utterly vague and hushed possibilities issue in a "breath": "The horror! The horror!" Marlow's own breath is at least more efficient in establishing, unambiguously, the darkness of the situation.

It may be obvious that the entire force of such episodes in Conrad depends upon the continuance of this "darkness," that his interests as a writer—at least at this moment in his career—depend upon or are reciprocal with "visual failure." It is not surprising, therefore, when his narrators explicitly avow their preference for the sounded presence of words over anything that they might see or understand through them, even while lamenting the loss of the latter in the discovery of this preference.

> "There was a sense of extreme disappointment, as though I had found out I had been striving after something altogether without a substance. I couldn't have been more disgusted if I had travelled all this way for the sole purpose of talking with Mr. Kurtz. Talking with. . . . I flung one shoe overboard, and became aware that that was exactly what I had been looking forward to—a talk with Kurtz. I made the strange discovery that I had never imagined him as doing, you know, but as discoursing. I didn't say to myself, 'Now I will never see him,' or 'Now I will never shake him by the hand,' but, 'Now I will never hear him.' The man presented himself as a voice." (112)

Or rather, Conrad presents him as a voice, and Marlow anticipates him as such. We have already seen in an earlier chapter how the vocal presentation of language constitutes the readiest access to its grammatical condition and possibility, and Conrad leaves no doubt that this is the mode of his fiction, that his narrator's interest in the "possible explanations" of his story generates a peculiar "atmosphere" of "meaning" at the expense of any visual imagining. "The yarns of seamen have a direct simplicity, the whole meaning of which lies within the shell of a cracked nut. But Marlow was not typical (if his propensity to spin yarns be excepted), and to him the meaning of an episode was not inside like a kernel but outside, enveloping the tale which brought it out only as a glow brings out a haze, in the likeness of one of these misty halos that sometimes are made visible by the spectral illumination of moonshine" (48).

Such "meaning," it should be clear, is not at all what Wittgenstein would call meaning, but more properly the "experience of meaning" that is produced by multiple and "surrounding" implications. We may be reminded here, indeed, of Wittgenstein's conception of the "atmosphere" of a word, its "'corona' of lightly indicated uses," like a "figure in a painting . . . surrounded by delicate shadowy drawings" (PI, p. 181). But we should note as well that Conrad, characteristically, conceives the "glow" that brings out this "haze" as itself insubstantial, "spectral." It is the moon that is at the center here, a source of light that is itself illusory because that light is reflected or even, as in Nabokov's derivation from Shakespeare's "pale fire," stolen. And this conception resonates with all the others in "Heart of Darkness" that figure the putative hearts or centers of the story—of Kurtz, of the "pilgrims," of the natives, of the jungle, of human life and morality—as not merely reflective but empty, "hollow." At the level of imaginative refraction upon which this narrative thrives, all images simply deteriorate, or vanish.

Of course, "Heart of Darkness" might seem a loaded case with which to demonstrate Conrad's thorough devotion to verbal conditions that make visual imagining impossible, though *Lord Jim* provides another example just as effective, and though similar motives may be seen to persist, even if not so undilutedly, throughout his career. But such a demonstration is not necessary here, for the "thoroughness" that I am trying to illustrate is not a historical but a technical or formal one, in which the proliferation of meanings that is characteristic of grammatical displays becomes so intense and complex as simply to eclipse the visual, where "saying" may utterly overwhelm "imagining."

But now I want to return to the less extremely grammatical situations in which the visual imagination is not so completely written out, where it is rather complicated and compromised, and where, because of a more balanced and complex relation between obvious visual features and displayed grammatical forms, the invitation to visualize seems more energetically extended. The undoubtable master of techniques that both generate the temptation to take a grammatical presence for a visual one and prevent us from acting upon it, of crafting "images" that both can and cannot be seen, once again, in my judgment, is Stevens:

> Among twenty snowy mountains,
> The only moving thing
> Was the eye of the blackbird.
>
> (*WS*, 92)

Again, there may be no difficulty in visualizing the parts of this sentence, the "snowy mountains," even if not exactly twenty of them, and a small, bright eye. But there would seem to be a problem in organizing them into an entire image. And so if one claimed that he could "see it all," we might want to ask him if he were perhaps not mistaking an evident grammatical "organization" and presence for a visual one.

The simplest problem here is one of visual scale and perspective. What single "picture" could contain twenty snowy mountains and a blackbird's eye? One might think of a "surreal" superimposition of pictures—some extravagant sort of double exposure—but that would appear to generate more possibilities and so more problems. Is that eye in a head, and by virtue of what contrast of light and color would it then be visible? And now one might even begin to speculate on the type of blackbird—redwing, grackle, crow, and so on—that was needed to accomplish a proper picture. But after all, it is difficult to estimate how far this shuffling of representational techniques would go, given the problem created by the pivotal line, by the fact that the blackbird's eye is "moving."

What seems most important, however, is not only that in such a case we are *thinking* of how to imagine rather than imagining, not only that the "visual possibilities" multiply here in a way similar to the proliferation of meanings in grammatical displays, but also that their tension against both the necessary singularity of a visual image and the evident grammatical wholeness of the sentence that generates them produces, again, a quite noticeably strange effect. As with the ball that one could "see" as shining and gold but only "know" as "hollow," one can "know" what this sentence says, but one cannot see with the singularity with which one knows. And so, in this play between knowing and seeing, or in the gap or hesitation between them, two or more images might seem, once more, to superimpose or to merge. Or it might seem that one's "imaginative focus" shifted very quickly from one to the other, and that in the intervals the "residues" of both images seemed to mix. But one might posit all sorts of feelings here, and think of them as descriptions of some imaginative "process," and I am not trying to choose among them. Only two features of this imaginative action seem to me clearly probable: that one shifts among various techniques for organizing an image, and that a perceived grammatical wholeness or organization may "carry over" and generate a visual "unity" that is quite unstable.

Even this degree of "imagining," however, may require a certain balance between apparent visual potential and verbal organization. For sometimes visual resistance is stronger, or grammatical unity weaker. As often as they seem to be unstable, the "images" produced in these situations may disintegrate immediately, may seem just to be mistakes:

> A man and a woman
> Are one.
> A man and a woman and a blackbird
> Are one.
>
> (*WS*, 93)

The first sentence of this stanza has all the grammatical inertia of the cliché that it is, the hypercoherence of a folk saying. It therefore obviates not only any imaginative "seeing" but also perhaps any other response except a passive or even a complacent acknowledgment. But the ostensible expansion, and dissolution, of this sort of coherence in the second sentence brings particular visualizing very much into question, as if one were now required to support the verbal with the visual. And, in that fruitless effort, one probably will not go so far as to imagine a tripartite sexual encounter, or a man and a woman in domestic partnership—say, at breakfast—with a blackbird, before giving up. For the unimaginableness of the second sentence may overexpose the "coherence" of the first and remind us that it, too—and this indeed was initially the source of its indiscriminate power—does not yield any single picture. So that its smug comfortableness now, from this visual vantage, seems unwarranted, since it provides no ground whatever even for trying to "imagine."

Cases like this one, in which the presumed weight of an expression—"a man and a woman are one"—depends upon the *exclusion* of visualizing responses, may reveal that our impulses to imagine upon what we say, to take verbal forms for visual shapes, are often so obviously mistaken as to amount for us to jokes. They may therefore be dangerous to try to explain. But it seems safe to say at least that this sort of joke, as so many are, is grammatical. It points up a grammatical divide, an unbridgeable gap between two modes of linguistic behavior, and between two altogether different sorts of "imagination." It is no wonder that the "image-mongery" that results from mixing them up—as Finch has suggested—makes us think of cartoons, whose game so frequently is to ask, "What if we could see *all* the things we say?" And that the effort to do so is grossly mistaken but nonetheless absurdly sustained by the visual techniques of the cartoons themselves is perhaps the main source of the comedy.

But it is one of the most interesting features of these situations that a joke about our language seems so often a joke on us, on the people who use the language. It is as if this humor at our own expense was to acknowledge—despite all our postures to the contrary—that our own language is often beyond us, that we are used by it as often as we use it, and that our engagement with it may anytime be revealed to exceed, easily and obviously, any actual applications even while we seem impelled to try to make them, and, in these present cases, to see the unseeable.

> I have also heard that he is in Cuernavaca in a deep trance of some two or three years' standing, and I have heard that he is not in a trance but is living alone in a small downtown hotel in Monterrey,

> wearing a beret, calling himself Principato and claiming to be five hundred years old. They say he looks six hundred, with his body all dried up from the desert air. They say he's all head now like a catfish and just tapers away to nothing. These are some of the rumors I have heard.[4]

Charles Portis is utterly brilliant at displaying such absurdities. The most outlandish or outrageous "visual" moments here alternate with and even are couched in a comfortable, droning, somewhat weary grammar, with its attendant familiar sounds, whose very conventionalness founds all of the jokes. So that the sources of the humor seem to shift away from its more obvious peaks, where nothing fits with anything—a man who is "all head," a catfish who is "all head" ("Some of them are!" one might say, before that "image" itself "just tapers away to nothing"), such a man like such a catfish—and through perhaps even more funny but more muted expressions—"a deep trance of some two or three years' *standing*"—to solemn declarations like "they say he looks six hundred" and finally, and simply, to "they say." (Consider, for instance, how important to the effect of the sequence is "These are some of the rumors I have heard.") Therefore, we might infer that the real joke here is on "them," on all those people who would say such things.

But that, I suggest, would be to disregard that we might say them too, to disregard our own attraction to these wonderfully ridiculous phrases, which may be hardly less thorough than their speakers'. It is this verbal acceptance of the visually unacceptable, the way we may be drawn to unimaginable expressions, that I find most interesting in these cases. For it seems a kind of revelling in language's capacity to exceed any experience that might be visually comprehensible for human beings, not merely an acknowledgment of that capacity but a courting both of it and of the "mistakes" in which it implicates us. In these cases our human manipulations of verbal possibility—here the ingenuity of Portis's writing—are revealed to put us in humanly impossible positions, so not only is any joke here at our expense, but we are also quite agreeable to the transaction.

The "mistakes" in question, in other words, are grammatically inevitable both because of how obviously our "saying" exceeds our "seeing" and because we frequently invoke its power to do so. So that even when certain speakers or their ways of talking seem to be singled out for ridicule, our engagement with what they say includes us in the comedy. "Lamar was a little surprised to find his own name on the list. It was given as 'Mr. Jimmerson.' His gossiping neighbors in Skokie, it seemed, had put him down for an odd bird. They had observed him going into his garage late at night in a pointed cap and had speculated that he was building a small flying machine behind those locked doors, or pottering around with a toy railroad or a giant ball of twine."[5] Here, I would suggest, the price of resembling those "gossiping neighbors in Skokie" seems low enough in exchange for being able to say "pottering around with . . . a giant ball of twine," and to discover—as if by deliberately running into a door that was closed—how visually inconceivable that expression ultimately is, despite whatever evanescent flashings of cartoon images it might generate.

But of course we may not always be such willing participants in this sort of game. That will depend, for one thing, upon the particular qualities of the "sayings" with which we are presented; and surely we shall be more inclined toward "they say he's all head now like a catfish" than toward "[they say] a man and a woman are one." But the unimaginableness of "what people say" is sometimes not merely unengaging but quite repulsive. The most obvious examples that I can think of are the headlines of the tabloid "newspapers" one cannot fail to notice while standing in line in supermarkets, where some vehicle like the *Star* or the *Enquirer* proclaims such things as "Siamese Twins Born Pregnant." In these cases we may have no desire at all to associate ourselves with such "propositions." Yet these instances are worth considering for a moment, despite their repugnancy, in relation to two questions. What makes them so ugly, so much expressions that one would *not* want to say? And what does their peculiar "unimaginableness" tell us more generally about the relation in our behavior between saying and seeing?

In answer to the first, we might say that they are simply "ugly language"; they are bald and blatant, with none of the rhythmic grace or fluency or culmination of "pottering around with a toy railroad or a giant ball of twine." And we might also propose that, despite their weirdness or ostensible adventuresomeness, they actually lack "imagination," that there is something common and boring about their insistence upon linguistic excess. This would suggest that certain restraints and refinements are necessary to such grammatical play, and, for example, to Portis's genius for it.

These features and others we might discover, however, seem to me traceable to a more fundamental accounting. These tabloid headlines are *not* offered as "sayings" at all; their "blatancy" stems from their pseudo-"empiricalness," their pretense to be assertions or observations about how the world, somewhere, actually is. And therefore they prompt a ready denial that would be, at least, delayed if they were presented as examples of what people will sometimes say. In this way we may see how important the condition of "grammatical display" is to the action of unimaginable language, how one may immediately reject weird phrasings that are not offered as sayings but as descriptions, whereas their presentation as human expressions would, again at the very least, postpone such a response.

Such "descriptions," we might react, cannot be descriptions at all; what they propose could not ever be seen anywhere; and this brings us back to the second question: how do we know that? What is our ground for rejection? Is it that "Siamese Twins Born Pregnant" is "biologically impossible"? It would seem doubtful that we worked this out in our minds at the moment of encountering the expression. Or has it already been worked out? Is the unimaginableness here the function of a disagreement between this "conception" and some presumed "facts of life"? Perhaps so. But such "facts" have themselves a double aspect. There is philosophical question as to whether we should regard them as "empirical"—"the way things are"—or "grammatical"—the way we customarily talk. But no matter how these "facts" look to us in isolation, it is certainly clear that usually they are what we presuppose or presume in our talk; and therefore they are, usually, grammatical principles or rules.[6] So that the "biological impossibility" of the *Star*'s or the *Enquirer*'s or the *Globe*'s Siamese twins is most likely a matter of grammar.

Of course, the boundary between grammatical possibility and "probability"—the difference between what people "can't" say and what they "don't" say—is not always a clear boundary.[7] But if it is likely that we shall regard "Siamese Twins Born Pregnant" more extremely, as "impossible" rather than "improbable," that is because of a grammatical collision—a too obvious and too fundamental collision between this expression and "facts of life" that no one would contest. Such a collision, once more, would be at least momentarily averted if, merely by the addition of a qualifying "they say," the strange phrasing seemed *proffered* as a matter of grammar.

To note, furthermore, that "they say" functions in these cases as a valve to relieve "empirical" pressures is also to acknowledge that it amounts as well to a license to apply such pressures as one sees fit. This is not a paradox. Language offered as language is free to a *play* of application as more assertive expressions are not; phrasings offered explicitly as grammatical examples grant us more applicational options, more ways in which we might stretch what we can see toward what we can say.

If this perpetual visualizing effort, this part of our double response to "grammatical" offerings—to odd expressions presented as such—now seems to indicate that it is not language in these cases but seeing itself that is our dominating concern, we need only remember the other side, remember that in such instances it is language's disengagement from application that makes us want to "see" in the first place. Therefore, this motive may be part of the more general disposition that I described with regard to "voice" when I suggested that no matter how grammatically remote expressions might seem—given that they *are* "grammatical," are presented as *sayings*—we are always trying to hear in them a "local sound." The attempt to see images under the most adverse or unpromising conditions may be part of some characteristically human penchant for trying to *apply* all of the language that is given to us as language, a disposition so habitual with us that, once again, when it is clearly mistaken, we find it comic.

This inclination to maintain the visual pressure upon the verbal is reinforced, in our experience, by two very different sorts of situations. In one of them, the effort to "picture" a strange saying may turn out, from time to time, successfully. There turns out to be, after thinking about it, a case somewhere in which the words in question form an imaginable whole, a context in which their syntactic organization produces or matches an image. Certainly searches of human experience occasionally may convert the unimaginable to the imaginable.

The other sort of visual encouragement is provided when "image-mongery" has been conventionalized by "representational" resources like cartoons, science fiction, and fantasy. So that one can have images of cartoon figures doing impossible things, or of space monsters, or of mythological beasts. But this is a very different sort of imaginability having nothing to do with applications to experience. It involves a quick and easy recourse or even "reference" to a conventional picture of a certain sort, a picture inseparable from a presupposedly special grammar. Imagining here depends and even is focused upon *techniques* for imagining, which is to say that to "have an image" of a unicorn is—and must be—to have something that would need to be described as a picture of a picture, and this is different from what we ordinarily mean by "having an image." One might call this sort of imagining—as I did in the introduction—"forced imagining," for it is "forced" either in the sense that we must resort to special techniques in order to imagine or in the sense that we shall be compelled to invent such techniques for the occasion.

Through both sorts of situations, then, through both empirical and grammatical developments, the range of the imaginable expands; the imaginable world keeps changing in at least these two different ways. As Wittgenstein, especially in *On Certainty*, sometimes cautions, what we presume imaginable at any moment depends entirely on the way things stand at that moment. And given the potential and probability of change, given the ways in which grammatical conditions may both become and seem to become those of experience, our confidence that we can imagine what we can say may seem to us justified.

But these "reinforcements," as I see it, are merely that; for the most fundamental stimulus to the effort to see what is said would seem simply to be the shape of the saying itself, a grammatical shape that appears to compose a visual one. No matter how we distribute the motivational weight here, however, the results of these interactions between the grammatical and the imaginable, as we have seen, may be strange perceptual "alloys." For even when there appears to be an obvious shift of force within a grammatical display toward the more singularly visual potentialities of words, the domination of the grammatical is such that what we may then see is much more, and much less, than an image:

> It was evening all afternoon.
> It was snowing
> And it was going to snow.
> The blackbird sat
> In the cedar-limbs.
>
> (*WS*, 95)

That thirteenth "image," perhaps, may really *seem* to be one. It could hardly be more immediate, more sharply relieved against the much less visualizable, much more essentially grammatical presences of the preceding verses, of the twelve other "ways of looking at a blackbird" that were rather demonstrations of or questions about imaginative techniques and procedures than presentations of singular images. And against the active multiplicity, against the imaginative motion, of earlier conditions, this last image also seems substantially at rest. But still it participates in, and is inextricable from, the grammatical activity that precedes it. It would do so, I think, even if it was itself more purely "visual." But as the last verse stands, its first three lines reinvoke and reinforce the apprehension of an unseeable terrain in which images and implications multiply rather than reduce, and where temporal locations already contain or amount to their own future and continuance. And thus the "image" of the last two lines continues, and becomes more than a perception within local space and time, and seems an augury of its future forms. Again, because one both sees it and knows more about it than he is seeing, one also seems to see more. Such an "image," in this way, is both an image and an idea, both physical and metaphysical—a continuing "image" that one could never lose and, therefore, an image that one does not really have.

Of course, even though this sort of experience is not the same as "having an image," we might call it "imagining" too. We do in fact employ this concept with this sort of looseness in literary studies, and "imagining" from time to time may cover any shapely experience that seems to depend only upon—or to occur only within—the mind. Paul Ricoeur provides an interesting definition of "imagining" that might justify such expansions of the concept. "To imagine, then, is not to have a mental picture of something, but to display relations in a depicting mode" (CI, 144). "To display relations in a depicting mode" is suggestive, and among its various implications it might describe the "grammatical displays" with "visual features" that I have been considering. But such an inclusive conception neglects—indeed, denies—the simpler "mode" of visualizing. Surely the most fundamental sense of "imagining" is "to have a mental picture of something" (or, in Wittgenstein's more careful and accurate phrasing, to have something that could be efficiently represented by a picture); and to deny that in our reading is to disregard, among other things, the productive tensions between single images and the more complex and "metaphysical" ones that I am treating here. These tensions are generated by the coincidence of obvious grammatical multiplicity and visual urgency, and they result in something that one seems both to know and to see, "presences" that are more verbal than visual, but that may seem to waver on a border between the two. Then, as with Wittgenstein's shining gold ball that we know is hollow, we may seem to see at once a composite or combinational image, or to see all the aspects of an object simultaneously: to see, in other words, with both the comprehensiveness and the singularity of grammatical apprehensions. "Aspected images" of this sort—to the extent that they are achieved as images—may seem to "flicker," to shift sequentially from one shape to another so quickly that these shapes appear to combine.[8] And perhaps that is also true of the multiple possibilities of words perceived in their grammatical condition; perhaps we would say that we can only think of one meaning at a time, while knowing that there are many meanings of which to think. But this "grammatical perception" *seems* more singular than that. Language in this condition, as we have seen, seems to contain its possibilities all together and at once; and it is this felt simultaneity in the language, I have suggested, that founds complex or multiple "images," that urges us to try to see—or to think that we can see—many images in one.

It may be that this sort of visual or imaginative "experience," as Wittgenstein says, can only be intelligibly claimed for dreams; we may continue to want to say—and this will depend upon further arguments—that anywhere else it is an illusion. But even so it is a *grammatical* illusion. Therefore, it may be inferred either that grammatical apprehensions can generate experiences something like those of dreams or, more determinedly, that dreams are themselves grammatical and involved in their special way with such apprehensions. And we shall be inclined to choose the second inference, I think, if we consider that, in Wittgenstein's terms, the "experience of meaning" itself—a grammatical phenomenon—is best conceived as dreamlike, or that the "fictitious natural histories" that he sometimes constructs to show what grammatical possibilities do not obtain in our actual experience often take the form of dreamlike fantasies. But either way, this perspective on dreaming may prove illuminating for literary studies in a way that more reductive conceptions—such as Freud's, for example, in which dreams are just another form of interpretable imagining—have not been. For if both dreams and certain varieties of literary expression are entwined with the grammatical conditions of language, whether or not in just the same way, then even the differences here will tell us something about literary experience. Perhaps more important, this connection can increase our more general appreciation of the reach and force of the grammatical both in and out of literature, and reveal more clearly our vulnerability to what we say, within whose vital possibilities we are so often and so intensely bemused.

Afterword

These arguments can scarcely be brought to a conclusion here. Whether or not I have been correct in them, they amount to an attempt to pose certain questions about language in a way quite different from those preoccupying most current literary theory. My hope is that the conceptual scheme engendered by these questions may prove valuable not only in describing the kinds of verbal form that I have identified as "grammatical displays," but also in discriminating among an entire range of other texts, from expressions that are devoted to showing the human importance of their forms of expression to those that instead say something—or, as we often put it, are "about" something—by pointing away from their own forms toward other words.

Solely within literary theory, this terminology has the capacity for many applications that I have not performed, not least because some of them seemed to me, as they will doubtless seem to others, so readily performable. But I hope as well that the same terminology may be useful in ways I have not imagined. For the way of describing linguistic expression that I have derived from Wittgenstein's ideas of grammar and "idling" language is not offered only as an announcement of the ubiquity of grammatical exhibits to one effect or another, nor even only as a clarification of certain literary critical confusions characteristically generated by such verbal forms—though this has been important to me—but also as a conception of verbal behavior at large that might easily, it seems to me, be extended to provide an accurate measure of language's varying modalities.

Even within the most obviously "grammatical" range of language use, there are all sorts of ways in which language displays itself, to a multitude of different effects, in literature and everyday talk. For even when an expression works altogether to expose its form, and is not a strange mixture of the "logical" and the "descriptive" of the sort we have noted in Hemingway, what is thus exposed and deactivated is some mode of working language, and language—as Wittgenstein has shown—can work in many ways: not only in many descriptive or "empirical" ways, whose grammatical conversions may be most dramatic, but also to many other purposes whose imaginative potential is revealed in their "grammatical" presentation.

Thus, when we see that an expression is not functioning in some meaningful way, we may have just begun to consider its effect, and everything interesting may remain to be seen, in the way of further description. My primary concern in these discussions has been to demonstrate that the "grammatical" resistance to meaning is an access to language in a different condition, and to turn off the "no exit" signs that have seemed, especially in recent times, to light up when doubts about the meanings of texts have arisen. I have tried to show that the very question of meaning—as Wittgenstein gives us to understand it—may be of great practical interest but does not fit other engagements of language that we mistake for it, engagements that are so puzzling mainly because we attempt to measure them on a scale of meaning, when in fact they are ways of attending to—and sorts of fascination with—language's grammatical forms.

Of course, we can give the language of a text only as much attention as that language will bear. For surely not every verbal set is working to "show language off" in some way, not every text functions to expose its form and to generate an experience of that form. There are plenty of texts—in literature and elsewhere, and of course the question of whether they are "literature" or not is *not* settled by the consideration of how they work—whose language functions assertively and even "empirically" and so does not support the concentration or focus that we give grammatical expressions.

I have said relatively little in these discussions about this more "propositional" sort of verbal action, for the characteristics of grammatical expressions—of "idling" language—seem to me much more influential, undiscovered, and confusing. But I now want to turn for a time to the question of how such "empirical" language works, for such an account—though I must be brief about it—may both further illuminate, by opposition, the qualities of grammatical expressions and give some shape to the other side of the conceptual range I have in mind.

We know from Wittgenstein that the grammatical-empirical distinction is a difficult one, for it cannot always or even often be made by examining the way an expression is constructed. "I am inclined to believe that not everything that has the form of an empirical proposition is one" (OC, 308). And he therefore suggests that the difference in question is often a function of how an expression, regardless of its particular grammatical composition, is *treated*, of its *role* in a verbal sequence. "It is clear that our empirical propositions do not all have the same status, since one can lay down such a proposition and turn it from an empirical proposition into a norm of description" (OC, 167). What we might do, then, because it seems easiest—for a "laid down" expression, even if not exactly a sitting duck, still looks more manageable than one in motion—is to begin with grammatical language and then try to discover, against that concept, what the characteristics of empirical language are.

But even if this way looks easier, it is still obviously a circuitous route. Why not just say what empirical language is? If it is the empirical that describes the realities of our experience, then surely this is the mode of language most familiar and fundamental to us, and most easily exposed. Yet it is unlikely, as I have already suggested, that the larger part of our verbal behavior, perhaps contrary to Wittgenstein's wishes, is devoted to meaningful descriptions; however "fundamental" it may be, it is unlikely that empirical usage is most characteristic of the way we most frequently talk. And even if it were, I think we shall see that describing the empirical against the grammatical will prove to be more than merely an argumentative convenience, because, as I shall try to show, empirical processes actually *work* by opposition to grammar, against the evident revelation and presence of grammar that we otherwise invoke in grammatical displays.

The proposal that grammar is involved, in some way, in empirical discourse might normally be nothing but a redundancy. But given what we have observed of the tendencies of grammar to *display* itself, and of our own inclinations to expose the grammar of so many of our linguistic engagements, the question of how a so determinedly self-devoted and static set of verbal conditions might be put to work to *describe* things becomes interesting.

To suggest that grammar is always with us, in *some* status or other, is not, however, to certify the by now commonplace notion that our language is inescapable, that we cannot "get outside" it to confront "reality." I shall try to show in a moment that "empirical" verbal processes *characteristically* seem to situate us if not "outside" words then at least somehow "between" them. But for now I would rather say that, much of the time, language is indeed "present" to us. We accentuate and emphasize this presence, once more, by means of continual grammatical demonstrations and exhibitions, by "laying down" language to each other. And it may go without saying that the most interesting occasions of our doing so are literary ones. But even if language is not so obviously dominating in working, descriptive, empirical expressions, it may seem something like "inescapable," because we always seem to end up with it.

"Look at that tree over there. It's a copper beech." Surely that, occurring in actual speech, would most often be an empirical observation; but where is the "reality" in it? For what we are brought up against here, when we *think* about it, is the *concept* of "copper beech," and so we are back with the grammatical again, and even in what appears a simply empirical gesture we have not "got outside" language. We may thus be led by such examples into an error; we may say that all verbal expressions, even empirical ones, "refer" to other language, and that when one points out or points to some "reality" one is merely pointing to other words.

But is that what I was doing when I pointed, by means of words, to the copper beech? Was it the *phrase* "copper beech" that was important? If so, then why did one turn his head to look? Why not just nod and muse upon the language? The problem here, I think, is that just in the citation of the phrase, just in thinking for an instant of this remark as a remark, it has got "laid down," and its grammatical aspects—as a pretty phrase, as a definition, as something I could *say*—have been foregrounded.

What needs to be recognized, however, is that in its functioning, perhaps for just a moment of its functioning, at the moment when one turned his head to look, "copper beech" was not exposed as a phrase but instead was *working* as a stimulus for someone to do something. And it worked that way because the conditions of its utterance—the most obvious of which was the timely action of a change of language, of saying something *different*—distracted one from the linguistic quality of the utterance. When one turned his head to look, "copper beech" was not a phrase but part of an action.

That action, I want to say, is the "reality" in such cases. What is unverbal about our experience is the momentary doings with which we respond to language. And in those doings, words are not present, not "laid down" as they are when their grammar is exposed. Language, then, once we have it, as a rule may be always with us—*except* for those moments when it functions by deferring to actions, when its identity as language is overlooked. Thus, if we want to say that empirical language "refers" to the world or the objects in it, we should understand that such reference is not a state of correspondence between words and things, but a much more active matter. Language may refer *us* to realities, may generate the action I am trying to describe, but it does so only by masking its identity as language with verbal change and difference. And therefore, at any empirical moment, the verbal half of the "correspondence between language and reality" is missing. "Referring" here—this "pointing to" realities—is before anything else a pointing *away* from words by means of words; and in this action the pointer must and does, for an instant, vanish. It is in this never more than momentary disappearance of language that the world—or the perception of an unverbal world—is produced. This is not to contradict Wittgenstein's claim that we always "see" through concepts; it is to specify further that, in our more empirical verbal behavior, we see through concepts by seeing against them.

It is worth saying, then, that everything that happens happens in relation to or by means of language, so long as we remember that such relations and means may be of very different sorts. The assertion, on the one hand, that "words refer to other words" even in empirical or descriptive processes only means that in these processes we are always eventually brought back to language. But in the empirical meantime, in the referential action, language is momentarily effaced; in the referential instant, we might rather be said to be between words.

In grammatical expression, on the other hand, words "refer" to other words much more obviously and directly, since by maintaining *their* presence and identity as language they invoke—or refer us to—other language as part of their systems of possibility. This self-exposure and self-sustenance of grammatical displays is sometimes characterized, altogether too loosely, in literary theory as a text's "self-reference," which can prevent us from seeing that what a text in its grammatical condition refers to are its implications of and connections with other vocabularies. As I have urged before, grammatical displays, even in their insistence upon their own formal qualities, are not local. They cut themselves off from working language or from meaningful vocabularies, but the "selves" that they exhibit in so doing are thus released to participate in all the grammatical possibilities that can be associated with them.

But the notion that empirical actions—these glimpses of "reality"—occur against and thus depend upon language, though in a way very different from the way of grammatical expressions, may come clearer if we think for a moment about the functioning not of abrupt and singular remarks but about verbal sequences. "The same proposition may get treated at one time as something to test by experience, at another as a rule of testing" (OC, 98). The implication from Wittgenstein that I want to press here is that the shift in status that expressions may undergo, the changes in the way they are "treated," is a *function* of their "timing," of their sequential positionings in a syntax.

Someone says, perhaps after a walk in the country, "The leaves have begun to change." That seems empirical enough. Its circumstances, which are implied by the tense of its verb, indicate its difference from what one had been saying, or could have said, about the leaves lately. (Verb tense—as well, of course, as mood—may be extremely important in making the grammatical-empirical discrimination, and sometimes it is an obvious indicator, except for many deceptive forms, such as the "grammatical present": "leaves change.") The "timing" of the expression in view within a probable sequence of other expressions thus reflects a temporal change outside it, which is another indication of its "empiricalness." At the moment of its expression, furthermore, it amounts to something "testable." Even if one did not go so far as to respond to it by looking out the window or taking a walk oneself, he could "check" it against other observations—the time of year, what the weather had been like, and so on.

But I am more interested at this moment in the way such empirical status can change, for this same remark may immediately become, if one continues with further description, a background or foundation for that description. If one next says, "The maples, especially on high ground, were changing more than the oaks," then "the leaves have begun to change" now functions not as an assertion but as a presumption that makes the next assertion sayable.

There has been some debate as to how to think of this change of linguistic status, as to what an assertion might be when it ceases to function as an assertion and becomes the condition for another that follows it—for example, when a move in a game is converted to the grounds for or even the proposal of another game. Some have said that expressions of this latter status are the "presuppositions" for those that follow, or even that they are "secondary assertions," as Max Black suggests, or "dummy moves," as in the contrast between setting out the pieces for a game of chess and the actual moves in a game (MM, 48). But I think—and this is why I prefer the concept of "presumption" here—that these and similar characterizations are still too "active," that they do not sufficiently recognize how radical the change of verbal state we are now considering actually is, how *unlike* "assertions" these backgrounded expressions actually are.

"In autumn the leaves of certain trees change color, some of them brilliantly"; that proposition is of a quite different sort from "the leaves have begun to change." Phrased as it is, it is an example not of immediate and occasional observation but of what we can always, anytime, say, and so it has its place within the definitions of "autumn," or of "deciduous trees," or even of "this world, the earth." It is a grammatical proposition, unquestionable, secured by the rules of how we normally speak. And its *non*-"assertiveness" may be confirmed by how strange it would be for someone to come in from a walk and say such a thing, how strange to say something that one could always say as if it were "timely."

But what I am suggesting here is that expressions that do not initially amount to presentations of the necessities of grammar—empirical expressions that mark temporary differences and that are "questionable" or "testable"—constantly achieve grammatical status in our speaking. And they do so precisely because further linguistic sequencing sets them aside or behind. The action of this sequencing is empirical, but what is passed and "past" in it becomes part of a grammatical background, part of what has been "given," just as securely as any more obviously grammatical proposition.

This helps to explain how the increments of differential verbal sequences—such as those in the most realistic prose fiction—take on such solidity after, and only after, the narrative movement has progressed beyond them. This substantialness is very like one of the sorts of "certainty" that Wittgenstein considers throughout *On Certainty*, a certainty that depends for its existence upon the *deactivation* of meanings to a grammatical state: "Much seems to be fixed, and it is removed from traffic. It is so to speak shunted onto an unused siding" (OC, 210). He is not speaking here, to be sure, of the way syntactic process continually establishes temporary or local grammatical presumptions, but of the more permanent sorts of "framework facts"—as H. L. Finch calls them—that are constantly taken for granted in our verbal behavior. But it is precisely the similarity in status and force between these latter, more perpetual grammatical constants and the former, occasionally and temporarily established grammatical presumptions that seems to me remarkable.

Still, even if these considerations help us to see how verbal sequencing converts empirical observations to grammatical presumptions—how the "treatment" of expressions depends upon their "timing"—they may not seem to answer the question with which we were most immediately concerned as to how those empirical observations "work" as such in that same sequencing. And yet they do. For the "traffic" here—the empirical *action*—is reciprocal with what is "removed from traffic"—with the *deactivation* of language. *Verbal* inaction amounts to *unverbal* action. "Empirical process" is the continual setting aside of language. We may think of this as a causal relation, in which grammatical solidifications cease, as they occur, to be of interest, and propel us onward toward others, which themselves cease to be of interest and cause more empirical motion. But we might say with as much accuracy that it is an "interest" in movement in the first place that causes, that indeed requires, the sequential deactivation of words. And this means that there is no "cause and effect" here.

It is interesting that this whole process that I am describing seems to involve a series of what might be called momentary "hinges," at which words first efface themselves in favor of action, and then reappear only in a suppressed, presumed, and grammatical condition, as if the light of language continually flared out and then rekindled into a more faintly lit but therefore more stable background. But whatever metaphors it provokes, what seems clear from the foregoing account, again, is that even the empirical process of language may be characterized as a certain regard or treatment of *language*, but of a very different sort than our regard for grammatical displays. The empirical and the grammatical modes, that is, both depend upon expressed attitudes—of perhaps opposite kinds—toward the fixations and presences that words in themselves accomplish.

In grammatical *expression* the grammar is exposed and presented as language itself, and the potential applications and actions of grammar are suppressed to the status of possibility, whereas in empirical discourse that same grammar is itself suppressed, continuously, into presumptive conditions that background and allow—and "rule"—actions. "Empirical language," therefore, is not as we sometimes may be led to think a different *kind* of language from the grammatical, for our descriptive or meaningful or more active concerns are not accomplished by language in some more flexible or timely or atomized condition. Verbal solidification is what it is: there is no solvent for language that makes it more "applicable" to experience. Language is always grammar, and so it is always at least potentially "present," and meaningful applications of language are only—broadly speaking—one way of *treating* grammar, which is to suppress and presume it.

Thus the assertion that language is always with us does not contradict the conception that empirical process is always momentarily unverbal, but underwrites it. For in our participation in such process we require words as something to set time after time aside or behind in favor of the next word, proceeding always both away from words and toward words. And this sort of reading, in taking its verbal material only as accumulating grammatical license for going ahead, seems itself unverbal, an action for which there are, at *its* moments, no words, and an "experience" of *that* sort.

We "see *through*," and past, words in one way, and this seems like "*seeing* through" them in another. But what we see through *to*, when we look at it, is of course words again. And when the differing process is sustained, when sequences simply continue until they stop, and leave us, as it were, "hanging"—as often happens, for example, in realistic fiction, or in traveling directions, or recipes, or countless other cases—then we are propelled toward other words outside them, toward vocabularies that we ourselves perhaps more usually presume and can use to ease the tension and fill that void, to "complete"—which, in one way here, just means "erase"—the differential process. And these terminal vocabularies we call, when we notice their formal difference from the processes that seemed to require them, "interpretations," or, when their otherness to what we have been reading is most conspicuous, "translations."

In this sort of case, then, one's attention to language is always very quickly extended past or through that language in the expectation of continuing applications that are supposed to be of more interest than language itself. One looks at language here only in order to look beyond it. And, of course, the more characteristically one is interested in potential applications and actions, then the less disposed he will be to attend to verbal features that compromise that sort of interest. This is to say that there may exist readers—like Frost's "eye readers," perhaps—who will want to "interpret" every text, or who will want to show that, by virtue of some "endlessly" differential action, every text is *un*interpretable in any singular way, these being the two sides of the same coin. And there may also exist readers who on the contrary so emphasize any text's recurrently formal features that it will always be converted into a "grammatical display" and have no determined application to anything but only the breadth of its resonance with other ways of talking.

Neither of these readers, in all probability, would be able accurately to recognize the complex cases that make up not only the majority of literary texts but also the greater part of verbal behavior in general. The first reader would not, certainly. Yet it is also clear that this first reader—like Wittgenstein's "aspect-blind" or "meaning-blind" man who has no *experience* of language—would be capable enough of performing quite efficiently and "correctly," so far as the singular application of any set of expressions is concerned. Something like the ultimate point of my larger argument, then, is that this reader for whom language must only be functional—purposefully, practically meaningful—is missing a great deal of what language often amounts to for human beings, missing even, as Frost has it, the best part. Meanings and applications, and the "realistic readings" of language that provide for them, were of first importance to Wittgenstein in his immense effort to ease the philosophical difficulties generated by more "grammatical" expressions, and thus to dispel in philosophy the very kinds of illusions that literary interests so often court and foster. And such functional verbal action informs a sizable part of our lives from day to day. But it is not what we live for. And that, of course, is a grammatical proposition.

Notes

Introduction

1. H. L. Finch, *Wittgenstein, The Later Philosophy* (Atlantic Highlands, N.J., Humanities Press, 1977), p. 154.
2. Anthony Kenny, *Wittgenstein* (Cambridge, Mass.: Harvard University Press, 1973), p. 45. Further references will be given in my text as *W* with page number.
3. *Wittgenstein and the Vienna Circle*, shorthand notes of F. Waisman, ed. B. F. McGuinness (Oxford: Blackwell, 1979), p. 92.
4. "It's as if the one who pronounces the sentence as a piece of information told us something, but as if the sentence too, as a mere *example*, did the same." *RPP* 1: 1091.
5. This is why the inference—which flowered decades ago but still flourishes in "deconstruction" and other literary theories—that certain sorts of literary expression are "about" language or their own form, and "say" something, or comment ironically, upon their own mode of construction, is so misleading. This may become obvious in various particular cases that I shall consider later. But for now one might simply suggest, as I think Wittgenstein has shown, that a picture cannot represent, or "say," anything *about* its form as a picture; it cannot get outside itself, so to speak, to do that. And displaying or exhibiting its form—which it can do—is a quite different matter.
6. Quoted in Kenny, *Wittgenstein*, p. 53.
7. This is in part a logical point: we cannot consider "hidden" or "secret" what could never be found or revealed.
8. "Freudian Slippage," *Raritan* 8, 1.

Chapter One

1. G. P. Baker and P. M. S. Hacker illuminate this point by characterizing the relation between rules and their applications as "internal": "If the method of application

is a bridge between a symbol and what it symbolizes, it is at any rate not built until the application is made. It is not the interpretation that builds the bridge between the sign and what is signified or meant, only the practice does that. It is not rules, of their own accord, that 'determine' meanings, it is the way in which we, in our activities, use rules, that does so. *Scepticism, Rules, and Language* (Oxford: Blackwell, 1984), p. 52. The entire discussion here of Wittgenstein's conception of rules seems to me most accurate and valuable.

2. At those moments, at any rate, where he would allow the *distinction* between "thoughts" and "language" necessary to such a relation. For often he draws our attention to their apparent inseparability, or perhaps to a relation that is extremely close: "Language is itself the vehicle of thought" (PI, 329). "Likewise it wouldn't be completely wrong to call speaking 'the instrument of thinking.' But one can't say that the process of speaking is an instrument of the process of thinking, or that language is, as it were, the carrier of thought, as, for example, the notes of a song might be called the carriers of the words" (RPP 2: 8). Wittgenstein usually insists that thought is not an "accompaniment" of speech—because not so separable from it as an "accompanying" relation would require—but he also says: "Sometimes it really seems that thinking runs concurrently with talking (reading, for example). Not that it could then be isolated from reading, however. Rather, what accompanies the words is like a series of small secondary movements. It is like being led along a street, but casting glances right and left into all the side streets" (RPP 2: 208). These and many other related conceptions, however, are complicated by the variety within the concept of thinking itself, which must result in this sort of acknowledgment: "You must never forget that 'think' is an everyday word, just as are all other psychological terms. It is not to be expected of this word that it should have a unified employment; rather it is to be expected that it doesn't have it" (RPP 2: 194).
3. PI, p. 181. A less elegant but more pointed characterization of how multiple "meanings" seem present to the mind—and do not merely exist as a background of *grammatical* possibilities that contrast with some singular meaning in "experienceless" operation—is as follows: "But there is the phenomenon that when a word is heard outside any context—for example—for a fleeting moment it has one meaning, and the next moment another; that if one pronounces the word over and over it loses all 'meaning'; and so on. And here it is a matter of something's *coming into one's head*" (RPP 1: 167).
4. "It would be just as wrong to use an experience of meaning to explain the concept of understanding meaning as to explain reality and unreality by the experience of unreality, or the concept of the presence of a human being by the feeling of a presence. One might just as well try to explain what check is in chess by a check-feeling" (RPP 1: 155).
5. He is clearer on this difference—or at least the difference with which I am con-

cerned here is clearer—in other remarks composed during roughly the same period as part 2 of the *Investigations*: "Why should the experience of meaning be important? He says the word, says he said it now in this meaning; then, in that one. I say the same. This obviously has nothing to do with the ordinary and important use of the expression '*That's* what I meant by this word.' So what is the remarkable thing? That we say something of this sort? Naturally that is of interest. But the interest here does not depend on the concept of the 'meaning' of a word, but on the range of similar psychological phenomena which in general have nothing to do with word-meaning" (RPP 1: 358).

"If anyone says 'Just now I spoke the word in isolation in *that* meaning,' he is playing a totally different language-game from someone who tells me he meant *this* by this word in that report or order.

"And so now it is either essential, or inessential, that he also uses the word 'to mean' in the first case. If it is essential, then this first language game is a reflection of the second one.

"Say, as a chess-game on the stage may be called a reflection of a real chess-game" (RPP 1: 1055).

6. This problem too seems more surely handled in typescripts contemporaneous with part 2 of the *Investigations*: "Then how am I to describe this psychological phenomenon? Am I to say: one can mean a word in such and such a way upon request? that one fancies one means it this way or that? Am I to say that the word 'mean' is being used here in a different sense; that one ought properly to have used a different word? Am I to propose such a word?—Or is just this the phenomenon, that we use the word 'mean' here, which we learnt for another purpose?" (RPP 1: 685)

Here, the conception that "mean" is learned for a more basic and practical *purpose*, and later must serve a different purpose, seems better than suggesting that in cases of *experiencing meaning* the sense of "meaning" is "figurative." And this conception also nicely parallels Wittgenstein's claim that verbal *competence* is a precondition for verbal *experience*, with no implication that the priority in question is anything but temporal, merely a matter of the order in which humans tend to learn what they learn.

7. I mean that it will be dangerously misleading for those literary theorists and others who may not be sufficiently aware of the derivation and background of this concept, and who might suppose—since games are presumably "fictitious" in a certain way, or even "nonserious," and have rules, etc.—that "language-game" is naturally a "literary" notion. Wittgenstein surely would not have had such readers foremost in his mind, nor should he have, and the severity of my remark is not aimed in his direction. But a reader familiar with Wittgenstein's arguments will nonetheless observe that his use of "language-game" here goes well beyond even the "liberalness" of the concept that I noted earlier, toward a sense that was previously excluded from it. And yet, in writings contemporaneous with the sec-

ond part of the *Investigations*, Wittgenstein sometimes uses "language-game" *both* for meaningful verbal actions and for grammatically "literary" ones: "This hangs together with the problem of 'meaning.' For I can write 'I am healthy' in the dialogue of a play, and so not *mean* it, although it is true. The words belong to this and not that language-game" (*RPP* 1: 933).

Chapter Two

1. *Word-Music* (New Brunswick, N.J.: Rutgers University Press, 1980).
2. The tragedy of Hemingway's career, for example—and I do not mean the personal and domestic tragedy of it, but what in my view was a remarkable artistic decline beginning with *For Whom the Bell Tolls*, and subsequently relieved only by too infrequent returns to his earlier style—seems to me the inevitable result of how he came to talk to himself about his writing, of the simple, mystical, "realistic" terms that he misapplied to the complex combination of motives and effects in his early work. And to believe, as I do, that he learned this jargon from what other people—literary hacks, for example, and absent-minded professors—were saying at the time about his work just makes matters worse. One's inclination to blame "them" only reminds one of how vulnerable the best art can be to inferior influences—something about which Hemingway, of course, reminded himself fiercely all the time—so that it would almost be better if one could think him alone responsible for the corruption of the magical narrative forms that he invented.

Chapter Four

1. Here I should say that for my purposes the difference between "metaphor" and "simile" matters even less than it did to Aristotle. Such a difference may in certain contexts be quite important, but it is also, in the abstract, easy to oversimplify. It has been supposed, for instance, that simile is logically more "literal" than metaphor, since it is more explicit in proposing likeness. But the opposite, as Davidson suggests, is also true: for when the more "economical" combination of terms in a metaphor inclines toward a conceptual relation, the presence of "like" or "as if" between these terms can maintain their difference, and insist upon the figurativeness of the juxtaposition. (This becomes clear as well in Max Black's remarks about "*as if* thinking" in "Models and Archetypes," *Models and Metaphors* [Ithaca, N.Y., 1962], p. 228.) The difference between metaphor and simile, then, must be described from case to individual case; and that holds true for all the differences among the specific varieties of metaphor defined by classical rhetoric.

   I am ignoring all these particular differences in favor of considering a more general grammatical action and condition that all sorts of metaphors, similes, and so forth generate in some way or to some degree, and what I have meant and shall mean by "metaphor" in this discussion is any grammatical construction in which two disparate elements, two terms from different verbal systems or vocabularies, are combined so as to impinge upon each other or, more specifically, to come into conflict.

The part and section numbers for Aristotle's *Rhetoric* that I have used here are the same from edition to edition.

2. *The Structure of Complex Words* (Norfolk, Conn., n.d.), p. 347.
3. *Models and Metaphors*, p. 46. Further references to this book will be given in the text as MM. Black's conception of the "interaction metaphor" is set against the more traditional idea that a metaphor always has a primary ("Achilles") and a secondary ("lion") subject, and that the secondary subject is only important in showing the primary one in a new light, and that it does so while remaining itself unchanged. But Black suggests—and seems quite right in doing so—that both terms of a metaphor are affected by their conjunction, that our reading of each is shaped by the presence of the other—hence, the "interaction." This is a view that is shared, I think, by almost every important commentator on metaphor in the last half-century or more.
4. *Critical Inquiry* 5, no. 1 (Autumn 1978): 32. Further references to this essay will be given in the text as CI.
5. Ernst Cassirer, *Language and Myth*, trans. Susanne K. Langer (New York, 1946), pp. 91–92.
6. Philip Wheelwright, *The Burning Fountain* (Bloomington, Ind., 1954), p. 96.
7. Joseph Katz, ed. *The Portable Stephen Crane* (New York, 1969), p. 399. Further references to Crane's work are to this edition and are given by page numbers in my text.
8. "Something monstrous lurks in the most innocent of catachreses: when one speaks of the legs of the table or the face of the mountain, catachresis is already turning into prosopopeia, and one begins to perceive a world of potential ghosts and monsters." "The Epistemology of Metaphor," *Critical Inquiry* 5, no. 1 (Autumn 1978): 21. That one only "begins to perceive," and that these monsters are only "potential," is important; though this was not a sufficient qualification for Locke, since de Man continues by citing Locke's warnings against such metaphorical illusions, against "*ideas* of substances disagreeing with the real existence of things," "chimeras."
9. "The Metaphorical Process as Cognition, Imagination, and Feeling," *Critical Inquiry* 5, no. 1 (Autumn 1978): 147. Further references to this essay are given in the text as CI.
10. *Lolita* (New York, 1955), p. 157.

Chapter Five

1. *Wittgenstein, the Later Philosophy*, p. 144. I shall suggest later that the concept of "cartoon imagery" here is more important even than Finch suggests, that this "mere

imagining" depends upon artificial *techniques* of "picturing," upon—as I shall maintain—"having a picture of a picture." To put this bluntly: if one *did* "imagine" a mouse writing a sonnet, it would have to be Mickey Mouse—or something like him—and not the one who rustles in the pantry at night.

2. "I can see the schematic cube as a box, but *not*: now as a paper box, now as a tin box.—What ought I to say if someone assured me he could see the figure as a *tin* box? Should I answer that that isn't *seeing*? But if he couldn't see, could he then *sense* it?

   "Of course it would be plausible if we said to him: Only what can really be seen can be *visually* imagined in that way. (Knowing in dreams.)" *RPP* 2: 492.
3. "Heart of Darkness," *Youth, Heart of Darkness, The End of the Tether* (New York, 1984), p. 82. Further references to "Heart of Darkness" are to this edition by page number..
4. Charles Portis, *Masters of Atlantis* (New York, 1985), p. 204.
5. Ibid., p. 17.
6. What I am calling "facts of life" here, H. L. Finch calls "ordinary certainties"—which he later also terms "empirical certainties" and "framework facts"—and his interesting description of them may explain my own inclination to consider them to be at least as "grammatical" as they are "empirical": "sentences which express these ordinary certainties appear to have a dual character. On the one hand, they are what we rely upon, what we take for granted, what stands fast; but, on the other, it is only in connection with specific situations, where doubt may enter, that the same sentences really tell us anything or convey any actual knowledge. It is as if what we are most sure about stays in the dark and is only illuminated when some unusual situation challenges it. *When we affirm or try to establish the truth of such certainties in isolation, without the illumination of the odd situation, they seem to lack sense*" (*Wittgenstein*, p. 223; my emphasis). I would rather say that what these expressions lack when offered in "isolation" is not "sense" but "meaning"; that is, they lack application, since their customary role is to form the presupposed grammatical background for more "empirical" assertions.
7. "But if by 'bluish yellow' I mean green, I am taking this expression in a different way from the original one [the "combination" of red and green]. The original conception signifies a different road, a no *thoroughfare*.

   "But what is the right simile here? That of a road that is physically impassable, or of the non-existence of a road? i.e. is it one of physical or of mathematical impossibility?" (*RPP* 2: 425)

   Earlier, Wittgenstein suggests that what is "impossible" is strictly a matter of grammar, whereas the "physically impossible" is rather, "properly speaking, not probable" (*RPP* 2: 199). One might suggest then that we say "impossible" in *empirical* cases merely for emphasis, and the proper expression would be, perhaps, "highly improbable."
8. The best figure to illustrate the simplest variety of this phenomenon, for me, is

not Wittgenstein's "duck-rabbit" sketch or similar line drawings, but his example of the octagonal shape that includes a black Maltese cross on a white ground and a white cross on a black ground; here it seems that one may see either one, as if by a certain "organization" of the mind that feels "conceptual," and also that one may oscillate very quickly between them. But it also seems that one may see something else, as if this figure—isolated from the application toward a single image—was itself an "image." If it is, however, it is a different sort of one, and not at all the same as those single aspects that seem to jump from the page when one determines upon them.